THE
GOLDEN GURU

Watch for other coming Golden Guru Books

The Golden Health Guru
The Golden Management Guru
The Golden Marketing Guru
Real Golden Guru Stories
The Golden Relationship Guru

THE
GOLDEN GURU

10 Spiritually Based Principles
to Success, Fulfillment and Wealth

Greg Roadifer, MBA

THE GOLDEN GURU
10 Spiritually Based Principles to Success, Fulfillment and Wealth

Published by: GoldenHouse Publishing
P.O. Box 23307
Billings, MT 59104

This book is sold with the understanding that neither the author nor the publisher is engaged in rendering legal, accounting, or financial services. As each financial situation is unique, specific questions and situations are individual and should be addressed to an appropriate professional for proper evaluation and advice.

The author and publisher specifically disclaim any liability, loss, or risk, personal or otherwise, which is incurred as a consequence, directly or indirectly, of the use and application of any of the contents of this work.

Publisher Cataloging-in-Publication Data
Roadifer, Greg, 1970-
    The Golden Guru: 10 spiritually based principles to success,
    fulfillment and wealth / by Greg Roadifer. - 1st ed.
    p.cm.
Includes index.
ISBN 0-9700414-3-8
    1. Self-actualization
    2. Success - Psychological aspects
    3. Personal Finance - Psychological aspects
    4. Wealth
    I. Title
BF637.S4.R63   2001
158.1-dc21   00-190933

To my boys,

*Trey Alan Roadifer
and Ty Hayes Roadifer—
I Love You and I hope this
book teaches you to value
yourself and to find your
golden mission in life.*

CONTENTS

INTRODUCTION

The median net worth in America is less than $15,000. Just 4% of the people own half the country's wealth, and 60% of Americans are unhappy. Why, in this land of riches, are millions of people failing to fulfill their dreams of internal happiness and external wealth?

This episode of *The Golden Guru Book Series* attempts to answer this question by teaching the basic laws of life fulfillment and wealth. *The Golden Guru* is a short parable written about six people—a spiritually oriented money expert named Sophia Plato (aka the Golden Guru), her friend Professor Braeburn, and their four students: Mark, Satya, Elena, and Gregory—who gather for an intimate seminar on money and wealth. By the end of the book, the Golden Guru and Professor Braeburn have taught ten simple yet sound principles for achieving total wealth.

Although all ten principles are spiritually based, the first five deal specifically with internal wealth and living a successful, fulfilled and spiritually balanced life. Four others deal with external wealth and focus on money and finances. The tenth and final principle offers a combination of success, fulfillment, and external wealth. As the teachers make clear, it's the combination or balance of all ten that brings true, total wealth to your life.

As the author, I have included many outstanding references and resources for further growth on these principles. I hope you will take the practical knowledge you gain from this book and expand on it. As with anything in life, you must intently study and take action on that which you want to achieve. Take my ten principles, study and use them in your daily life. As a result of your increased knowledge and action, you will acquire the confidence to accumulate an abundance of success, fulfillment and wealth.

THE STORY

Professor Braeburn sat at his desk at the university, evaluating student papers. Although he had been teaching for more than twenty years, he still enjoyed seeing how his students integrated and applied what he had taught them. The phone rang, and when he picked it up, he was pleased to hear the voice of one of his favorite former students. The young man, whose name was Gregory, had landed his first management job, and he was eager to thank his former mentor for the guidance he had received from him.

Gregory had also recently discovered Professor Braeburn's Golden Guru Book Series. "Your books are full of some incredible ideas," he told his teacher, "and I'm eager to put them into practice. Unfortunately, none of the books focus on personal financial success. You know, the basics, like how to make more money and how to manage the money I have. I hate to admit it, but my goal is to become wealthy as quickly as I possibly can."

Professor Braeburn smiled to himself. "Yes, of course, for many people money seems to be the bottom line. I'm planning to write a 'Golden Guru' book on money and wealth, but I haven't gotten to it yet. When I was your age, I too was extremely interested in amassing wealth. In fact, I managed to make a small fortune during my first ten years as a professor. Now I can retire whenever I want, but I love teaching so much that I'm in no hurry. The person I have to thank for my knowledge of money matters is a wise, spiritually centered person who taught me the simple principles that govern wealth when I was fresh out of graduate school."

"Who was that?" the young man asked, intrigued.

"Let's just call her the Golden Guru," Professor Braeburn replied enigmatically. "Although I haven't written the book yet, I do teach the wealth-building strategies I learned from her. In fact, she and I generally teach them together. This Saturday morning we're starting a small wealth-building seminar for a few of my former students. Perhaps you'd like to join us."

"I'd love to," Gregory replied, pleased with his timing. "Where is it happening, and what time will it start?"

"In my office at nine a.m. sharp. It will be great to see you again," said Professor Braeburn. "I must point out that we teach wealth and money a little differently than most. We first focus on valuing yourself and living an internally wealthy life."

"I look forward to it," Gregory said with excitement. "Thank you."

Gregory arrived at the professor's office about a half hour early the following Saturday. As he approached the door, he could hear laughter coming from inside. He knocked tentatively.

"Welcome," said the professor as he ushered Gregory in. "I'm glad you could make it. We were laughing about all the mistakes I made when I was learning the basic wealth-building principles. I was incredibly stubborn, and I found it hard to let go of some of my preconceptions. But we'll talk more about my mistakes as this seminar unfolds. As I like to say in my business classes, you can learn as much from the mistakes of others as from their successes."

"Yes, I remember you repeating that phrase many times," said Gregory with a smile. "It is definitely one of your well used golden oldies." All three chuckled at this quip. "But I can't tease you very much as I've found that piece of advice to be incredibly helpful." He revered

Professor Braeburn and looked forward to this opportunity to learn some insider secrets from him.

"Now let me introduce you to my guru," Professor Braeburn beamed, turning to a woman sitting in the armchair next to him. "Her name is actually Sophia Plato, but I like to call her the Golden Guru because she's taught me so much about fulfillment, success and money."

As Gregory stepped toward her, she rose and took his hand.

"This is Gregory Allan," Professor Braeburn said. "He's one of the best students I've had in recent years."

"Very nice to meet you," said Sophia, gazing directly into Gregory's eyes.

Her strong, sensitive, unflinching gaze and the silver-blue color of her eyes took the young man by surprise.

"Pleased to meet you," he mumbled.

The Golden Guru was of an indeterminate age, with golden blonde hair and deep feminine beauty. Gregory could also sense a strong spiritual presence. She seemed to radiate spirituality, truth, and love. *I guess that's why they call her a "guru,"* he thought to himself.

Soon other students began appearing at the office door: first Satya, an earthy Indian woman in her late 30's who had gone back to college to study with the professor after her kids had reached school age. Then Mark, a thoughtful, introspective computer programmer who had taken the professor's courses as electives while completing his degree in computer science; and finally Elena, a friendly, articulate woman in her mid-20's, who was finishing an MBA at the university and still actively taking courses with Professor Braeburn.

After brief introductions and some small talk, the participants settled into chairs in the large book-lined office, and Sophia opened the class by writing this headline on a marker board on the wall:

10 GOLDEN PRINCIPLES TO WEALTH

"Through many years of study," she began, "I've discovered ten basic principles that can lead an individual down the road to total wealth. As far as we've been able to determine, these principles are universal in nature. It doesn't matter if you're poor or rich, male or female, white or black, red or yellow. The truth is the truth."

"Are there really only 10?" asked Mark who was obviously excited about how easy the pursuit of wealth might be.

"Basic truths are often succinct and simple," smiled Sophia, "but, in the long run there is much more to learn after the first ten. These principles are what I consider the basic foundation to wealth and happiness."

Mark nodded and seemed content with the answer.

Golden Sophia paused for a moment for emphasis.

"Have you ever watched the construction of a house from start to finish?" she continued, glancing toward Gregory.

"Yes," Gregory offered. "My father is a teacher and coach for nine months of the year and a carpenter the other three. I spent several summers as a teenager helping him build garages, houses, and sheds."

"Wonderful," Sophia said, smiling to herself as she had done a bit of research on each student's background in an attempt to use relevant examples. "Tell me the first step in any new development or carpentry project."

"That's easy," Gregory said. "You have to develop a solid foundation to build upon."

"Exactly," Sophia cheered. "It's incredibly important to have a solid foundation to build on. Of the ten principles that govern fulfillment, success and wealth, the first five are extremely important because they form the foundation for the success of the last five. They are psychological, spiritual, or life-oriented in the sense that they don't deal with specific external wealth-building strategies."

"The first five laws have nothing to do with the green dollar bills," added Professor Braeburn. "Rather, they teach the importance of our behavior or attitude toward money and life. We call them the internal wealth principles."

Sophia began writing on the marker board:

10 GOLDEN PRINCIPLES TO WEALTH

Internal Wealth

1. **GOLDEN INTERNAL WEALTH**

"**W**ealth is a word with broad meaning that goes far beyond dollars and cents," Sophia explained. "The best definition of wealth I've ever come across was written by Peter McWilliams. I've expanded it quite a bit. Wealth is self-value, happiness, health, fulfillment, abundance, prosperity, riches, loving, caring, giving, sharing, learning, dreaming, achieving, opportunity, enjoying, success, pursuing our passion, and balance.

"Wow! Wealth seems to have a lot to it," said Elena.

"Clearly, internal wealth involves a lot more than money. It involves valuing yourself from the inside and living a full, rich life. To value yourself and to grow within, you need a healthy combination of love, happiness, giving, caring, learning, nature, balance, and a strong spiritual connection. Professor Braeburn and I will focus on giving you a solid understanding of internal wealth. We'll teach you why it's so important to strive for value deep within. In fact, over the next two weeks we'll teach you what we consider to be the most important principles for building internal and external wealth." She paused.

"We don't consider ourselves exclusive experts on the topic of wealth," she continued. "Many people have a great deal to offer. We highly recommend some excellent books that will help you understand wealth. We urge you to read *The Five Rituals of Wealth* by a young financial expert named Tod Barnhart; *The Instant Millionaire* by a great author named Mark Fisher; and the must-read classic *Think and Grow Rich* by Napoleon Hill. Also, you must read Suze Orman's books, such as *The 9 Steps to Financial Freedom* and *The Courage To Be Rich*. We urge you to read these excellent books because they'll help you grow wealthy both internally and externally. Throughout this course we will often recommend great works on the topic."

Sophia nodded to Professor Braeburn, and he picked up where she left off. "When I was young and poor, I thought wealth meant cash, preferably in $100 bills." Everyone laughed. "Now, after years of reflection and study, I understand that wealth is not just money, real estate, or stock certificates—it's a way of life. Wealth, internally speaking, is an emotion or value within. You must feel wealth inside. You must sense that there is absolute abundance inside yourself as well as in the economy."

"I totally agree," added Sophia enthusiastically. "It's crucial to understand that I could give you a million dollars, but it wouldn't make you a truly wealthy person. Internal wealth must start with a complete appreciation for who we are as individuals and for the miraculous world around us. We must have an awareness of the perfect spiritual energy that can be found in each and every one of us."

"Only when we begin to know that we are internally wealthy, which must include an appreciation for ourselves and for life, can we begin our journey toward external wealth. More money will not make us happy, peaceful, or wealthy. We only become truly wealthy when we're loving, living, learning, giving, and growing within."

Satya raised her hand. "You make wealth sound spiritual in nature," she offered. "In India we tend to separate the material and spiritual dimensions, but you're suggesting they may not be as far apart as one might think."

"Exactly," Professor Braeburn agreed. "Internal wealth is spiritual and love-based. The search for internal wealth must be an important part of our life mission. Fulfillment in life will come as you begin to feel spiritually connected and wealthy inside."

There was a moment of silence as everyone reflected on the implications of this teaching. Mark finally broke the silence with a question. "So what you're saying is that monetary wealth has little importance if I don't value myself and my life?"

"Yes, precisely," replied Sophia. "Now you're getting the drift. Most people think that money will solve all their problems. It's my duty to teach people how great money can be, but first they must learn how important it is to know love from within. When you're confident and comfortable within, you literally attract emotional, physical, and even external monetary wealth. Ultimately, fulfillment in life comes from your work within yourself, not the external or physical you."

"To develop a comfort or love inside," Professor Braeburn explained, "you must strengthen your spirit and soul. You can accomplish this through inner silence, prayer, reading, nature, music, the arts, education, or journaling from your heart. Or you can use exercise, meditation, yoga, hobbies—even watching powerful and positive TV shows and movies can help."

"This is a crucial point," the Golden Guru said softly. "Total wealth will only come from your state of mind and your ability to enjoy the world around you. Not only you, all people must develop peace within themselves. In essence, we must enjoy every moment of life as we reach for our goals and dreams.

"Think about it. Is life worth living if you can't find a way to value the person living it? People know they're good deep down. We must all find strategies to unearth this essential goodness."

"Write this down," said Professor Braeburn. "You must work harder on improving and developing yourself than on anything else you do. This is the most important point that either of us could ever teach you. If you work harder developing yourself, you'll become a better employee, a better friend, a better spouse, a better person in every way. Work on yourself to become wealthier inside and wealthier in your checkbook."

"I agree," said Sophia.. "I think that one of the key ingredients in a great life is knowing how important it is to continually work on yourself."

"I think I understand the importance of working on and valuing myself," Elena mused. "But how do I go about doing it? I mean, what exactly do I need to do to develop my internal wealth?"

Sophia paused for a moment and looked into Elena's eyes as if probing her soul. Finally she replied, "There are hundreds of different paths and directions a person can take on this search for true internal wealth and life fulfillment. The key is to listen to your inner intuition and do what you know is right. Search deep within and you'll find the peace, love, and bliss that lie at the heart of internal wealth."

"As we mentioned before," added Professor Braeburn, "prayer, meditation, reflection, education, music, hobbies, religion, reading, exercise, nature, yoga, writing, art, giving, listening, and learning are a few of the most common ways to begin your journey toward true internal wealth."

"Personally," said Sophia, "my favorite ways to grow are meditation, prayer, exercise, reading, and following my calling in life. Write these down, because in my pursuit of internal wealth I've found the work of Ken Blanchard, Deepak Chopra, Stephen Covey, Wayne Dyer, Jack Canfield, Mark Victor Hanson, Louise Hay, Napoleon Hill, Og Mandino, and Anthony Robbins to be especially valuable."

"I'm fond of spiritual classics like the Bible, *The Teachings of the Buddha*, the *Bhagavad Gita*, and *A Course in Miracles*," Professor Braeburn added. "Be sure to visit your library and bookstore regularly, and don't forget about the great used, religious, and Christian bookstores in your area."

"How does reading help?" Satya asked. "After attending classes during the day and taking care of the family at night, I'd rather spend my free moments sitting quietly and emptying my mind, rather than filling it with more ideas."

"I also strongly urge times of quiet and of emptying your mind. Sitting quietly, prayer, meditation and reflection are some of the most important strategies to growing your self-value. But, reading can touch your soul as well," Professor Braeburn answered. "Have you ever read any of the *Chicken Soup for the Soul* stories by Jack Canfield, Mark Victor Hansen, and others? They're very uplifting, inspiring and fulfilling."

"Yes," Sophia agreed. "I also love the *Small Miracles* books by Yitta Halberstam and Judith Leventhal and *Divine Interventions* by Dan Millman.

"Good books warm our hearts and enliven our spirit. Before you leave today the Professor and I will give you a list of some of the most influential materials we've read, listened to, or studied. If you like to learn and improve yourself and want to find internal wealth, success and fulfillment, you'll love the insights these experts provide.

"The second way I create internal wealth involves 20 to 50 minutes of exercise almost every morning. As I walk or jog, I visualize and meditate on my spiritual, personal, health, and career goals. This allows me to focus on my priorities at the start of each day. Your body and mind feel so energized after you exercise, even if it's just a 30-minute walk or a 20-minute Yoga session. If you don't exercise, you're missing out on a beautiful part of life.

"My third self-valuing technique is to pray or meditate each morning after I exercise to further help me get in touch with my spiritual side. Praying and meditation gives me a bliss or euphoria that no other activity can, except perhaps being in nature. You know the calm you feel when you sit next to a beautiful river, gaze at a sunset, or smell fresh mountain air. The only other time I experience this is when I pray or meditate."

"Don't forget about love and sex," said Professor Braeburn mischievously. A ripple of laughter broke across the room.

"Yes, love and sex can bring euphoria too," said Sophia with a raised eyebrow, "but we should probably reserve that for another class."

"My morning routine is similar to yours, as I do exercise," said Professor Braeburn, "but I use journaling as my main growth tool. I also add about 30 minutes to my morning routine so that I can listen to classical music, personal development tapes, or read spiritual literature. I do a different one of these each day, depending on what my heart and intuition dictate. As always, the key is to do what feels right for you."

"You must do the things in your life that make you feel good about yourself. Everyone is different, so pick your own growth tools, but you must grow inside," said Golden Sophia.

"Yes," nodded the Professor. "Find hobbies that you are passionate about. Hang around friends and family that make you feel good inside. Do things that improve this world, and find activities that help others. Basically it boils down to spreading love through the universe."

Professor Braeburn leaned back in his chair, put his hands behind his head, and took a deep breath. Outside the window of his office a songbird chirped enthusiastically. "All this discussion about growing within and reading spiritual material leads us to our next wealth-building principle. Principle 2 is a crucial component of self-valuing and inner growth."

Sophia wrote the next principle on the board:

10 GOLDEN PRINCIPLES TO WEALTH

Internal Wealth

1. GOLDEN INTERNAL WEALTH

2. GOLDEN SPIRITUAL CONNECTION

"**P**robably the best way to grow within or enhance a personal sense of value is to develop your spiritual connection," Sophia explained. "Most people sense that there is something inside us and in the cosmos, a spiritual energy, if you will, that's bigger than all of us. It's this something, or our search for it, that gives greater meaning and quality to our lives."

"Notice she said the *search* for this spirituality, rather than the complete understanding," said Professor Braeburn. "Even if you don't fully understand your spirituality, you'll begin to value yourself and life more if you start to think about, learn, or reflect on this part of your life."

"I'm sure all of you can recall times when you longed for meaning and purpose in life," Sophia said.

Gregory and Satya nodded silently in agreement, while Mark and Elena gazed wistfully into space.

"This longing inside can be filled by developing your 'golden' spiritual connection," Sophia continued, tapping on her heart. "I'm not here to sell you on a particular religion or belief, I'm here to urge you to develop your own spiritual path. I know that each person's path is unique. No one on the outside can tell you what you know on the inside. My recommendation once again is to sit in silence, listen to your intuition, read, study, pray, meditate, and search for the spirituality that's right for you.

"Don't just take my word for it; listen to what one of the most beloved and respected women in America says about these principles. Oprah Winfrey has met and interviewed thousands of people, from the very wealthy to the very poor, from the spiritually attuned to those who have lost their way in life. On a past broadcast she observed that virtually all the problems people face stem from a lack of personal value and spiritual connection.

"Essentially, Oprah concluded that the lost souls in this world are missing the two principles we just taught you. The most successful and fulfilled people have been able to (1) acquire internal wealth or self-value and (2) develop a strong spiritual connection."

"As we said before, spirituality is a personal matter," said Professor Braeburn. "Don't get scared by it; simply start investigating it. I'm going to give you a list of some of the 'golden techniques' that you can use to help you grow spiritually and develop your self-value and internal wealth."

GOLDEN GROWTH TECHNIQUES

1. Take a minute each morning to reflect on your own perfection and the perfection of the world around you.

2. Take a minute each morning to pray and give thanks.

3. Take a minute to reflect on the beauty of nature wherever you find it—in your backyard, outside your window, or on a walk.

4. Take some time for an early morning walk or jog. Breathe the fresh air and take in the healing energy.

5. Take some time daily to sit in complete silence and meditate, reflect, or pray.

6. Take some time daily to listen to inspirational or loving music.

7. Take some time for yoga or another healing activity.

8. Take some time every morning to listen to spiritual or personal development tapes.

9. Take some time each day to read, learn, and grow.

10. Take some time to do something good or to give to someone.

11. Take some time to visualize yourself living your dreams and goals.

12. Take some time to hug and love your family.

13. Take a minute every hour to take a few deep breaths, relax, and just enjoy being.

14. Send a silent prayer or compliment to everyone with whom you come into contact. Give the people around you some affection; after all, they're part of your world.

Mark, who had shown no emotion during the first part of the class, began to choke up as he said, "I really do want to value myself and feel good inside. I can be so hard on myself sometimes, so self-critical. Maybe it would really help if I spent some time praying, meditating, and reflecting on my spiritual life, as you suggest."

"Yes, I believe it would," Sophia said gently as she gazed lovingly into Mark's eyes. "Your inner self does want to love, learn, and grow. All you have to do is spend a few minutes each day searching your heart.

"In my own research," she continued, "I've found that many top business executives spend personal quiet time each morning or night thinking, praying, meditating, reading, or reflecting in an attempt to align themselves with their life purpose. Because spirituality is an intimate matter, many of these executives are reluctant to talk about this quiet time. But years of study have taught me that the majority of the truly successful and wealthy people in this world search daily to find peace within.

"Many people are financially wealthy and externally successful but don't have it all. The people that have internal wealth (which may or may not include external wealth) are the truly successful people. And the people who have both internal and external wealth are the happiest, because they are in perfect balance."

"Although times are changing, there still seems to be a stigma or embarrassment in our society about getting in touch with our spiritual side," Professor Braeburn observed. "Very few of us are taught as children the value of prayer, reflection, and meditation. In my classes I enjoy encouraging my students to go into their center and find truth, God, and love. The university administration thinks I'm rather weird, but they've never hassled me about it. After all, I'm not pushing a particular religion or spiritual perspective."

"Of course, there does appear to be a new movement emerging in the world toward more spirituality," Sophia added. "People are beginning to want more out of life than just material comfort."

"This may be a bit of an oxymoron, but perhaps we're moving into a technospiritual age," quipped Professor Braeburn.

For some reason, Mark found this comment particularly funny. "I'll give your 'golden growth techniques' a try, and maybe I can become a technospiritual pioneer," he said smiling.

"Hold on for a moment," said Sophia. "We haven't finished presenting our techniques yet. The next wealth principle highlights a technique that is so powerful it not only helps you develop self-value and wealth within, but it can also help you develop a 'golden' spiritual connection."

10 GOLDEN PRINCIPLES TO WEALTH

Internal Wealth

1. GOLDEN INTERNAL WEALTH

2. GOLDEN SPIRITUAL CONNECTION

3. GOLDEN GIVING AND RECEIVING

When she finished writing the third principle, Sophia pulled a plaque from her briefcase. "I'd like to read a poem that one of our students wrote several years ago. It's very simple, almost childlike, but I think it's an ideal way to start our discussion of 'golden giving and receiving.'

GOLDEN GIVING

We must give and give and give

to fully love and live.

Nothing feels better

than to send love, prayer, a flower, or a letter.

If we're looking for peace inside,

we must board this spiritual ride.

For it is the give and take in life,

that eliminates much of our day-to-day strife.

Giving circulates energy for all of thee,

and it helps to set us all free.

We must engage in this loving, harmonious exchange

if we want love, health, wealth, and positive change.

In addition to all this, it is those who ask and believe

that their wildest dreams they will receive.

"You're right, it's very simple," offered Satya, "but it has a charming innocence and it presents some powerful spiritual truths."

"I agree," added Gregory. "It feels good to give to others, but we so easily forget about giving in our efforts to take care of ourselves."

"Yes, giving is the best way I know of to find value and wealth within," said Sophia. "In fact, giving and loving are two of the most important things we can do in life. If we want to feel great about ourselves and continue to grow as individuals, giving is key.

"As this poem makes clear, giving not only helps you value yourself but it's also the first step in receiving. Basically, you must give to get."

"Yes," added Professor Braeburn. "In this universe there's a steady yet dynamic exchange of matter and energy—a harmonious flow of give and take, if you will. We take an active part in this exchange. For example, when we breathe, our body receives energy in the form of oxygen and gives it back to the world in the form of carbon dioxide. To live a vibrant life, we must continue to circulate oxygen and carbon dioxide. If we stopped circulating these gases, our bodies would die. The same thing happens with our food, thoughts, and even hidden energies that are much harder to define. On the spiritual dimension, we must continually circulate the energy of love in order to grow as individuals and as a planet."

"Most people don't think about this subtle spiritual dimension," Sophia added, "because we can't feel it with our five senses. It goes beyond taste, smell, touch, sound or sight. Many people sense it, but the sciences haven't really studied it because it can't be measured or quantified. For a great explanation of this dimension, check out Gary Zukav's super book *The Seat of the Soul*."

After a moment of silence, the Golden Guru continued, "Like love, wealth is a dynamic energy form that must also be circulated. Wealth is merely a symbol of the life energy that we give and get for services received and offered. The more we give to others and the universe, the more the giving circulates and returns to us."

"This principle works for both internal and external wealth," Professor Braeburn added. "Internally, I learned a great deal about giving from Deepak Chopra's book *The Seven Spiritual Laws of Success*. Essentially, he teaches that the more generous we are with people and the environment, the greater we value ourselves. Giving also allows us to be more connected to God and the spiritual universe. And giving doesn't necessarily involve money. We can give people tangible things like flowers, cards, gifts, or poems. Or we can give them intangible things like attention, love, affection, blessings, or a silent thought or prayer."

"Professor Braeburn and I have formulated an internal version of the Golden Rule," Sophia said, "which is to give something to every person you come into contact with, even if it's just a compliment or a silent blessing. By giving, you'll make yourself and the world a better place."

"Yes," Professor Braeburn agreed. "I send love to everyone I meet. If I'm in a room full of people, I send love to the entire room."

"But what if I don't feel generous or loving?" Elena asked, somewhat puzzled. "Sometimes I'm angry or worried or upset; what then?" Mark and Satya nodded in agreement.

"That's a great question," Professor Braeburn replied, smiling. "Naturally, you won't always feel like sending love. But if you just give, no matter how you feel, I can guarantee that you'll end up feeling better about yourself and about life in general. A great example is the movie with Robin Williams called *Patch Adams*. I believe it is based on a true story. Once Robin's character Patch figures out the golden secret of helping others, he moves from daily depression and begins to value himself and his life at a much higher level. He goes to medical school and then creates an incredible healing facility. He creates a facility that has much more life and feeling than many hospitals. His life takes on great meaning when he begins to give of himself."

Elena sat quietly for a moment, taking in what Professor Braeburn had said. "Thank you," she said finally. "I have a sense of what you're describing. I'll give it a try."

"The same principle works with external wealth as well," Professor Braeburn continued. "With external wealth I've learned that the more we give of ourselves, the more the money comes. If we give more hours, more intelligence, more knowledge, or more value to our customers or employers, the universe gives us more in return.

"Why do you think some people are paid more than others? It is because they're perceived as being more valuable to the business or organization. If you want more, you have to give more—it's that simple. Check out Jim Roan's books and tapes. I heard him discussing this 'increase your own market value' idea on *The Peoples Network* TV program the other day, and he really makes sense."

"One important form of giving that is often overlooked is tithing," offered Sophia. "Tithing asks that we donate a percentage of our money to spiritual organizations, such as our church or temple. You must read Mark Victor Hansen's book *The Miracle of Tithing*. He's tithed for many years, and look what the world brought him—the incredibly successful *Chicken Soup for the Soul* series.

"If you don't want to donate to a religious organization, then find another deserving recipient and be sure to give in a spiritual and loving way. You'll certainly receive in return much more than you give. By tithing, you're supporting the flowering of spirituality in the world—and what could be more valuable than that?

"Probably the most important thing you can give to the world is the one thing you were uniquely born to give. Each of us has a life passion or mission (some people label it a 'calling') which, if we pursue it, will yield us abundant rewards. Giving our life to our passion, calling, or mission in life is an extremely important part of giving. If we all pursued our 'golden mission,' we would create a magnificent and dynamic world. We'll talk more later about finding our mission in life because it's our final wealth-building principle."

"Now we need to talk about receiving," said the Golden Guru, moving her open hands toward her chest to emphasize her point. "In addition to developing our internal wealth and spiritual life, we must open up inside to what life has to offer. To fully receive life's gifts, we must fully accept and love ourselves. Much of what I've learned about receiving has come from my favorite author, Dr. Wayne Dyer."

"Just know that you are a great person deep down inside," Professor Braeburn agreed, looking deep into the eyes of each of his students, "then work on bringing that person out. Don't blame your problems or bad habits on someone else; instead, accept full responsibility and tell yourself that you'll continue to improve and grow as a person. Once you know that you're worthy, you will listen closely to your intuition, and you'll begin to notice the significant events, people, and things that show up in your life. Gradually, you'll begin to understand that the universe is offering you everything you need to prosper.

"I am going to use a very personal example," added Professor Braeburn. "When I was younger, I was sexually abused. This abuse caused me to become somewhat of a rebel in my late teens. I even got messed up in drugs and went through depression. Finally, I realized that I would never get ahead in life by feeling sorry for myself. Everyone has personal and tragic events in their life. I came to understand that this sexual abuse ultimately made me a stronger person. I knew that if I could survive these events then I could accomplish anything."

Sophia interjected softly, "Feeling unworthy prevents the receiving energy from flowing to us naturally. This blockage may divert energies that can show us how to achieve our goals. We own our life and our feelings and many of us need to take more responsibility and use less blame. For example, by feeling unworthy you may exude an energy that drives away someone you were supposed to meet—someone who might have supported you with knowledge or money to fulfill your dreams. We must be open to receiving. Read Dyer's work!"

"One way to begin to receive is to enjoy the little things in life," said Professor Braeburn. "This may include noticing and appreciating the fresh air, sunshine, and flowers outside your window each day or the gifts of others, such as conversation, affection, love, music, movies, and art. We must open our hearts and enjoy life."

"I totally agree," Sophia said, nodding enthusiastically, her silver eyes gleaming. "Whatever life offers, including money, we must receive and say thank you. If you build up your self-worth and your spiritual connection and allow yourself to give and receive, you'll be well on your way to total wealth."

Everyone fell silent as they considered how they might expand their capacity to give and receive.

"I think 'golden' giving and receiving segues nicely to the next wealth principle, which is discovering exactly what we want in life," Sophia offered. "If we build up our inner wealth, develop our spiritual connection and learn how to give and receive, we're ready to discover what we want in life. Listen carefully, and we'll explain how."

On the board Sophia wrote the fourth principle:

10 GOLDEN PRINCIPLES TO WEALTH

Internal Wealth

1. GOLDEN INTERNAL WEALTH

2. GOLDEN SPIRITUAL CONNECTION

3. GOLDEN GIVING AND RECEIVING

4. **GOLDEN LEVERAGE WITH DREAMS, VALUES AND GOALS**

"**D**eep down in our souls," she said, touching her hand to her heart, "most of us know that our life has great purpose and meaning. We know we have something unique to offer to the world. I believe that all of us have dreams and visions for the type of life we truly desire."

"The problem is," Sophia continued, "our dreams and thoughts of purpose and individuality are often buried in the difficulties, frustrations, and distractions of life. Many of us no longer attempt to live a life of excitement and meaning. If you really think about this, I am sure you'll remember moments when your mind exploded with a vision for your perfect life, a sense of excitement about a career choice, or a sense of destiny and purpose.

"These dreams or visions may appear in our minds just for an instant. Unfortunately, most people allow them to slip away or be overridden by fears of change or negative thoughts and emotions.

"Wealth principle 4: Create golden leverage with dreams, values, and goals is crucial because it teaches us how important it is to create a plan or strategy to determine and master our personal and financial dreams. It helps us unveil our true purpose or passion in life and the reasons for pursuing it. Not only do dreams, goals, and values give us something to work for, they also will allow us to uncover other important things about our life, such as new dreams, goals, values, and relationships that we may have never discovered."

"Let me put this in more practical, down-to-earth terms," offered Professor Braeburn. "Gregory, when you and your father were building garages and houses, did you have a plan of attack?"

"Of course," Gregory said. "We always had a building plan or blueprint. Without a plan, any building project would be almost impossible to complete because you wouldn't know where to start. Without a plan you would almost certainly get lost and frustrated because you wouldn't know where to put the windows or walls. As I think about it, you even need a building plan or blueprint to lay the foundation. If you make a mistake on the foundation, the entire project could be destroyed. It just doesn't make sense to build without a blueprint or plan."

"Exactly," said Professor Braeburn. "And it doesn't make sense to develop your life without a blueprint or life-plan either. By creating leverage or a force in your life with focused dreams, goals, and values, you're developing and controlling the structure and purpose of your life. As with building a home, you need a blueprint or plan so you can develop a solid foundation on which to build. By giving your life direction and purpose, you'll be energized and empowered to create a life filled with meaning and joy."

"As Professor Braeburn says, dreams, values, and goals are very important," the Golden Guru agreed. "A well-defined purpose and a clearly written list of values, goals, and dreams are crucial because they set into motion all of an individual's power, energy, and momentum toward fulfilling those goals. The mind is a powerful organ that can draw upon opportunity, people, knowledge, experience, and infinite intelligence to best pursue what we ask it to do."

"Yes," Professor Braeburn concurred. "Deepak Chopra, the outstanding mind-body expert, points out in his bestselling book *Ageless Body, Timeless Mind* that wherever thought goes, a chemical goes with it. If you tell your mind to pursue a goal, a chemical travels through your body energizing your cells toward that goal."

"That's amazing," Gregory said. "I had no idea that setting goals had such a far-reaching effect."

"It does," Sophia responded. "The human mind, body, and spirit continually pursue what we think about. For this reason, it's extremely important for us to get clear on what we want. In so doing we prepare our minds and bodies to best absorb activity, energy, and intelligence around us so we can use it to the best of our ability."

"A good example is when I created my Golden Guru Book Series," added the Professor. "I was thinking and meditating daily about what I could do in my life that might make a bigger impact or reach more people. After intense thought I was jolted awake by a dream that told me to write the book series. My mind even told me the name and the direction. All this occurred because of my intense thought on the subject."

"One of the most important things we can do in life is to learn how to control our thoughts and allow our whole being to radiate our purpose. That is why Professor Braeburn and I spend a few minutes every morning feeling the pleasure we will get out of working toward our dreams, goals, and values. By visualizing our successes, we energize our minds and bodies to move in this direction. We give ourselves leverage from this focused intention. Most importantly, visualizing and reflecting helps us enjoy the path or process of striving for our dreams, goals, and values."

"My father and father-in-law were both dream-centered and goal driven, and they were both able to set and achieve many of their dreams and goals in life," Gregory mused. "I guess I know how beneficial dreaming and goal setting can be. I just don't know where to start."

"That's a good point," Satya agreed. "How do we go about determining our goals and dreams in the most effective way? I daydream all the time, but I don't necessarily find it helpful."

Sophia handed each student a list of quotes:

GOLDEN QUOTES

"Ask and you will receive. Seek and you will find. Knock, and it will be opened to you."

— Matthew 7:7

"The mind is a goal-striving mechanism."

— Maxwell Maltz

"You become what you think about all day long."

— Earl Nightingale

"Without visions, people perish."

— Proverbs

"Start with the end in mind."

— Stephen Covey

"We are what and where we are because we have first imagined it."

— Donald Curtis

"Nothing happens unless first a dream."

— Carl Sandburg

"Great quotes," Mark offered. "I'm especially impressed by the range of sources."

"Thanks," Sophia said, smiling. "We can learn a great deal from those who have gone before us."

"Would you explain how you go about creating leverage with dreams, values, and goals?" Sophia asked Professor Braeburn. "You've always been such an outstanding dreamer and goal setter."

"I've learned a great deal about dreams, goals, and values from you and from great authors like Ken Blanchard, Anthony Robbins, Stephen Covey, Charles Givens, and Richard Bolles," replied Professor Braeburn, leaning forward in his chair. "I'd be happy to pass on what I've learned."

"I would suggest starting with a dreams list," he said, looking around the room. "To make a potent dreams list you must imagine that you have unlimited time, money, and ability and you'll use these to fulfill your deepest desires. Here are three major categories we have set up to help our students focus and organize their dreams."

Professor Braeburn began writing on an overhead:

GOLDEN DREAMS

1. Spiritual/Emotional/Physical Dreams
2. Business/Career/Financial Dreams
3. Personal/Travel/Adventure Dreams

"You need to sit down, clear your mind, and write down everything you would ever want to learn, experience, or master," he continued. "Be a little crazy and have some fun with this. Write down anything and everything you would want if you couldn't fail and had all the talent, time, and money in the world. In fact, act as if you had just won a ten million dollar sweepstakes."

"May I offer a few examples that may trigger some dreams?" Sophia asked.

"Go right ahead," said Professor Braeburn.

"Remember, this is only a partial list," Sophia said as she handed each person a copy. Then she turned on an overhead projector and put the list up on the office wall.

DREAMS

I. Emotional/Spiritual/Physical

1. Who do you want to be?
2. What do you want to learn?
3. How do you want to feel inside?
4. How do you want others to see you?
5. What fear do you want to overcome?
6. How do you want to quiet your mind and connect with your spirituality?
7. How do you want to connect with nature?
8. What kinds of music will uplift and inspire you?
9. How will you create the body of your dreams?

II. Business/Career/Financial Goals

1. **What business can you improve and grow?**
2. **What invention do you want to produce?**
3. **Where can you create more value at work?**
4. **How will you create a business around what you love?**
5. **How much money do you want to have in the bank?**
6. **When do you want to buy that rental property?**
7. **How much will you save each month?**
8. **What investment program will you try?**

III. Travel/Adventure/Personal

1. What states or countries do you want to visit?
2. How many vacations do you want this year?
3. Where would you like to build your vacation house?
4. Where has your family always wanted to go?
5. What exciting and unusual activity would you like to pursue? Fly an airplane? Star in a movie? Skydive?
6. How would you like to express your creativity?
7. What kind of car do you want to drive?
8. What famous person would you like to meet?

"It's important to write down dreams without evaluating them or anticipating their effects," the Golden Guru advised. "Specific dreams may take a long time to achieve or may never be achieved, but they inspire or force you to take a path of intention. As you'll find out with our next wealth principle, intention or action is a key to fulfillment.

"Although you may never fulfill some of the dreams you write down," she continued, "these dreams may lead you to a new set of exciting dreams. This new set of dreams may be your real destiny, a destiny you may not have found if you hadn't created an original dreams list."

"A good example of a dream leading to a new and more exciting dream occurred in my life," offered Professor Braeburn. "When I was a boy, I had a dream of playing college basketball. This dream turned into a goal that I eventually achieved. While playing college basketball, I realized how much I loved being on a college campus where I could continue to learn and teach. My first dream developed into a new dream of becoming a college professor. Without my college basketball dream I may never have attended college.

"Once I became a college professor, I dreamed of writing personal and business development books, which led to my best-selling Guru Series. The moral to the story is that working toward one dream often leads to other exciting dreams and goals."

"I see what you mean," said Elena. "My dream of creating and marketing my own line of clothing led me to the MBA program here at the university. Otherwise, I'm sure I would never have dreamed of doing postgraduate work, especially in business."

"Yes, exactly," said Professor Braeburn.

"We're going to leave you for 15 minutes," Sophia said, handing everyone a lined sheet of paper. "While we're gone, imagine that you've just won the Publisher's Clearinghouse sweepstakes and have 10 million dollars to spend. Write down everything you would ever want and do with this kind of money and freedom. Remember, just write everything that comes to mind without judgment or evaluation."

When Sophia and Professor Braeburn returned, they were pleased to find that all four of their students had managed to fill their pages with wishes and dreams.

"Excellent job," Professor Braeburn said. "Remember that your dreams list may change and grow over time. Both Sophia and I continue to add to our dreams lists.

"Now that you have listed your dreams, the next step is to review and reflect regularly on this mix of dreams, passions, and desires. We suggest to our students that

Sunday is a great day to review your dreams. By reviewing them on Sunday you energize yourself for the week ahead."

"A focused look at my dreams each Sunday really helps me whip the 'it must be Monday' blues," Sophia remarked. Everyone laughed knowingly. Still laughing, she added, "Just wait until we get to wealth principle 10—it's the best cure for the Monday blues."

"Let's move on to values," said Professor Braeburn, eager to make the best use of their time. "We must dig deep into our hearts and souls to create a list of values that will center our lives."

"Values inspire us and form the basis for everything we do," Sophia added. "Values allow us to determine from the inside what we really value the most."

"I agree that values are important," said Mark. "I have a lot of values. But I guess I've never taken the time to determine what my most important values are."

The other three students nodded in agreement.

"That's unfortunate," said Professor Braeburn, "because getting clear on what's important can add worth and peace to a person's life. But don't worry, we can help you determine your most important values right now. First let me hand you each a typed copy of our golden values list."

GOLDEN VALUES

God	Giving
Love	Adventure
Joy	Creativity
Freedom	Power
Learning	Confidence
Education	Family
Health	Integrity
Peace	Beauty
Bliss	Humor
Passion	Respect
Excitement	Challenge
Honesty	Courage
Fun	Spirit
Communication	Independence
Intelligence	Religion
Personal Growth	

"From this large list you need to choose the five to ten values that you feel the most strongly about," Professor Braeburn instructed. "Please add others if you think we've missed some."

"We'll be right back," he added as he left the room with Sophia.

Several minutes later they returned with a pitcher of ice water and a bowl of fruit.

"Once you've selected nine or ten values, you need to get serious and narrow your list even further to around four or five, because most people can only concentrate on a few supremely important values," said Sophia.

The four students worked on their lists for several more minutes while Professor Braeburn and Sophia nibbled on some fruit.

"Everyone has a completely different list of values," Professor Braeburn explained. "Each of you is unique, and your personal values will be right only for you. Just to prove to you that each of you has different values, we'd like you to write them on the overhead."

Satya, Mark, Elena, and Gregory lined up and took turns writing down their values. Here's what they came up with.

SATYA	MARK	ELENA	GREGORY
Family	Knowledge	Freedom	Wealth
Love	God	Peace	Love
Health	Wealth	Religion	Family
Fun	Health	Love	Spirit
Abundance	Adventure	Health	Passion

"Do you see what I mean? Now, if each of us creates our own golden values list and follows it daily, we will be more effective and more centered," said Sophia with a smile.

"I agree," said Professor Braeburn. "Values are crucial when you make moment-to-moment decisions in life. Values give you a consistent foundation to rely on."

"Now that you have your values list, the next step is to spend a few minutes every morning and evening reviewing it," Sophia continued. "Both Professor Braeburn and I review our values list first thing in the morning and before we go to sleep. We both believe that it helps us stay centered on what's really important throughout the day and in our dreams as well."

"This leads us to our next topic: goal-setting," Professor Braeburn said. "Sophia and I review not only our values list every day but also our goals list. Anthony Robbins taught me to think of it this way: Finding true internal wealth and spiritual connection is a primary purpose or mission in life. Declaring our dreams gives us excitement and passion. Reviewing and living from our values provides a foundation for making decisions and taking action. Finally, our goals help propel us forward, give us feedback, and allow us to keep score in our lives."

"Goal-setting is important," agreed Sophia. "It not only gives us direction, but it also motivates us to get up and do something."

"I've also found that goal-setting gives me confidence, because once I know what I want I can set about accomplishing it," offered Elena. "I'd never have made it to grad school without clearly defined goals."

"I agree," said Professor Braeburn. "Clarity allows us not only to strive but also to become perfect receivers and translators of the information and energy that comes our way. When we are enlightened and focused, the body can become a powerful tool to help us reach our goals. We will listen more intently for clues that will help us reach our goals.

"Our goals fall into eight major categories," he said as he began writing them on the overhead.

GOAL CATEGORIES

1. Family
2. Career
3. Financial
4. Spiritual
5. Personal
6. Travel
7. Health
8. Friends

"To focus your mind and body on achieving your goals," advised Professor Braeburn, "we suggest that you limit yourself to only a few important goals in each category. When you're considering your goals in each of the eight categories, make sure they're what the author and speaker Ken Blanchard, with a slight variation of my own, calls SMART goals; specific, motivational, astronomic, relevant, and trackable.

"For a goal to be most effective, it needs to be clear and concise. To set your mind in motion, you need to be quite *specific* with the details of your goals. It also helps to set a time frame for reaching your goals and to read your goals out loud to yourself every day. You must release your goals to the world by writing, thinking and acting on them. Be specific and allow the universal energy to fit them in to the bigger scheme of life.

"According to Blanchard, your goals must also inspire and motivate you to action," continued Professor Braeburn. "The only reason we do things in life is to gain pleasure or avoid pain. Your goals need to offer you the prospect of achieving one or the other as a reward for your efforts."

"I'll take the next two," Sophia offered with a warm smile.

"You must set goals that are *astronomic*," she said, looking around the room. "Goals need to push and extend you, you must shoot for the stars. But, keep in mind that they can't be so unreachable that your mind gives up and turns off.

"Goals must also be *relevant*," continued Sophia. "They must be congruent with your dreams, values, and mission in life. We must focus on the goals that contribute to making us the person we want to become."

"Finally, we come to the T in Blanchard's acronym, which stands for *trackable*," Professor Braeburn concluded. "One of the main reasons we set goals is to create a method of keeping score. Put yourself on the path of your dreams by writing goals that can be used as a scorecard to success. Remember, though, that attaining your goals isn't always the most important thing; often, the path or journey toward those goals is even more important.

"I think it was Anthony Robbins who said that having dreams, values, and goals allows us to develop a magnificent obsession that will create a compelling future. Tony likes dreams, values, and goals because they allow us to grab hold of our life and squeeze the passion, power, love, energy, and juice out of it."

"I agree with Tony Robbins," said Sophia. "We all need to think about and clearly define our life so that we can create the energy and momentum to succeed. The power to get out of life what we want."

"We'll let you work on your goals in the coming week," she continued. "Just make sure that, when you create your goals, you formulate SMART goals. Right now we need to move on to the fifth principle that governs wealth. Once you've created leverage with dreams, values, and goals, you have to take another step and turn them into golden intention and action. To get everything you want out of life, you must develop intention and action."

10 GOLDEN PRINCIPLES TO WEALTH

Internal Wealth

1. GOLDEN INTERNAL WEALTH

2. GOLDEN SPIRITUAL CONNECTION

3. GOLDEN GIVING AND RECEIVING

4. GOLDEN LEVERAGE WITH DREAMS, VALUES AND GOALS

5. **GOLDEN INTENTION AND ACTION**

"**D**reams, values, and goals mean nothing to the world until you act on them," the Golden Guru said as she initiated discussion on this principle.

"Why do you think millions and millions of people have had billions and billions of wishes, hopes, dreams, goals, and fantasies that have never come true?" Professor Braeburn asked the group.

"Well, I suppose it's because they never did what they needed to do to turn their dreams and fantasies into reality," Satya responded.

"Exactly." Professor Braeburn clapped. "Your intentions and actions ultimately create your reality. In his book *Real Magic,* Wayne Dyer says, 'Intention is the energy of your soul coming into contact with your physical reality'. By intending and then acting, you give life to your goals and dreams."

"If you shift your mindset from wanting to intending,

which means making the commitment to do some-thing, the energy of the universe will align itself with your intentions, and what you intend will come to pass," Professor Braeburn explained. "The real secret to get-ting all that your heart desires is to shift to the active energy of intention and action."

"A good example of a shift to intention occurred in my life around the issue of health," said Sophia. "I used to dream about being stronger and healthier with a higher level of energy. I fantasized and dreamed about it for years. I even wrote it down as a goal. Nothing happened until one day I read about a 33-year-old man who had died of a heart attack. His death was appar-ently caused by an unhealthy lifestyle. For some reason, at that very moment, I switched from dreaming to intention. As I switched to intention, I actually got off my couch and went for a walk. When I came home, I was hungry for a snack. Normally, I would have had a candy bar, but these didn't appeal to me at all. Instead I craved fruit and a cold glass of water. My simple switch to intent actually changed what my body desired."

"Even more amazing is that a few days later two health books arrived. The first, *Make the Connection: 10 Steps to a Better Body and a Better Life* by Oprah Winfrey and Bob Green, came in the mail from a cousin I hadn't seen in a year. The following week a friend of mine sent me a proposal for a book he wanted to write with me called *The Golden Health Guru*. As soon as I switched to intention, the universe aligned itself and my intended reality started to occur. I never looked back, and now I'm healthier than ever."

"That's incredible," Gregory exclaimed. "It gives me the chills when I hear about coincidences like that."

"I know what you mean," Sophia said with a smile, "but you must realize that it wasn't coincidental at all. There's an intelligent universal energy force that can be harnessed by our power within. We're part of this energy force, and if we align ourselves with it, it brings us the objects of our desires. Your thoughts, visualizations, and intentions are your way of manifesting or attracting what you desire."

"Every morning and evening Sophia and I release our dreams and goals to the universe, with the intent that they materialize," Professor Braeburn explained. "The vast majority of our dreams and goals have become reality, some immediately and others more slowly. Those that haven't yet materialized were either not wholeheartedly intended or not furthered by consistent action."

"Sometimes we don't achieve certain dreams and goals as soon as we'd like because the universal intelligence is waiting for the correct time or venue to grant them," added Sophia. "The universe has a bigger picture in mind, and our goals and intentions will materialize only when and where they fit into this bigger picture. But of course you must first intend them and then act on their behalf.

"One person's work and consulting I highly recommend is Jay Abraham. Pick up his book *Getting Everything You Can Out of All That You've Got*. He has super real world examples of taking action in your career or business."

"If you want to learn about creating your destiny, I strongly urge you to read Wayne Dyer's book *Manifest Your Destiny*," said Professor Braeburn. "You won't be sorry."

"Now it's time to move on to the next four principles for achieving wealth," continued Sophia.

"These next four are less spiritual than the first five because they deal with external wealth, the actual dollars and cents aspects of wealth. After these four, the final wealth principle will bring us back to the spiritual side of life."

"Yes," Professor Braeburn agreed. "We've laid out the spiritual foundation for financial success; these next four principles will help you deal with the money. If you're able to master the first five, you're well on your way. But if you want to create wealth, you must learn and follow the final five principles as well."

"Absolutely the most important external wealth principle is the next one," said Sophia. "Number 6 is so important that it has been dubbed the Golden 10% Rule."

Sophia added the sixth principle to the list:

10 GOLDEN PRINCIPLES TO WEALTH

Internal Wealth

1. GOLDEN INTERNAL WEALTH

2. GOLDEN SPIRITUAL CONNECTION

3. GOLDEN GIVING AND RECEIVING

4. GOLDEN LEVERAGE WITH DREAMS, VALUES AND GOALS

5. GOLDEN INTENTION AND ACTION

External Wealth

6. GOLDEN 10% RULE

"For creating wealth as a beginner, no single financial rule is more important," she said emphatically. "I began my career as an entry-level manager of a large corporation. My income was respectable, but I knew I would have to combine hard work, a great deal of overtime, and much luck to climb to the top of the corporate ladder where the real money is earned.

"There were no guarantees that I would make it, especially given the glass ceiling for women in corporate America. With no absolutes in my career, I thought maybe I could become wealthy by budgeting and saving. I set out in an attempt to save almost every penny I made. By the end of one year, I had nothing to show for my efforts. There was always month left when my check ran out, so there was never anything to save.

"Since budgeting wasn't working, I made probably the smartest decision of my life. I turned to knowledge and education to get ahead. I realized that I needed to learn from people who knew what they were doing— people who had achieved what I wanted to achieve. If I wanted to learn how to accumulate wealth, I determined that I should read, study, and listen to material produced by experts who had accumulated wealth themselves.

"I spent several months after work and on the weekends in the library reading about the stock market, real estate, and many get-rich-quick schemes. It was all so complicated.

"Then I came across the book that changed my life. It was an old book, filled with simple truths about becoming financially independent. Its title was *The Richest Man in Babylon*, by George Clason. Babylon was an ancient city of great wealth and intelligence, and many of its inhabitants followed fundamental rules to financial success. No one knew or taught financial success better than the richest man in Babylon."

"With Sophia's encouragement, I too read *The Richest Man in Babylon*," said Professor Braeburn. "Some of the laws and rules that were taught in Babylon are the same ones we will teach you. Probably the most important law is what they called 'start the purse to fattening.' In ancient Babylon the wise were taught to pay themselves one coin out of every ten earned. The idea was to save a minimal 10% from the top of every paycheck."

"It seems so simple," said Gregory.

"Remember, great truths are often simple," Sophia replied.

"But people save all the time and don't get rich," Gregory countered. "I'm not convinced that saving a little money out of each check will make you rich."

"OK," Sophia responded after a moment of silence. "Let me explain it in a way you'll surely understand. How old are you?"

"Twenty-five," said Gregory.

"Now suppose you make $24,000 a year, and for simplicity's sake we pretend that you never get a raise. Let's assume that you want to retire when you're 65. If you invest $2,400 a year, or $200 a month, and you average a 15% rate of return per year for 40 years, how much money would you have for retirement?"

Professor Braeburn handed Gregory a calculator.

"Well, $2,400 dollars a year times 40 years is about $96,000 plus some interest," Gregory said after punching in some numbers. "I figure I would have about $200,000 at retirement."

"Nice try, but not even close," Professor Braeburn

said, laughing. "You should have taken my investment and personal finance course."

Gregory seemed a little embarrassed.

"Actually, the answer is $6,203,211," said Sophia gently.

"No way," Gregory whispered, incredulous. "You mean that two hundred dollars a month turns into . . . six million dollars?"

"Yes," Sophia answered. "In your calculations you forgot about the magic of compound interest. Every year your interest accumulates, and you earn 15% on an ever-higher figure."

"That's incredible," Mark interjected.

After a moment of silence Gregory added, "Well, I only see one problem: Where will I get a 15% rate of return?"

"I'll answer that question later," responded Sophia. "First, I'd like to ask Professor Braeburn to tell you a great story about his little brother, compound interest, and the Golden 10% rule."

"Gladly," said the professor with a bemused smile. "I taught my brother the same secrets to financial wealth that we're teaching you now while he was still in high school. He got really excited, but he didn't know how he could come up with even $75 or $100 a month to invest. I explained to him that the exciting part about starting when you're so young is that time is on your side. With time on your side you don't have to start with much money. Due to the magic of compound interest, you'll be surprised to discover what a minimal $50 a month will do for you.

"To make a long story short, my brother started investing $50 a month when he was 18 years old. If he continues to receive a 15% return on his investment of $50 a month for the next 47 years, or until he retires at 65, his money will grow to over $4 million dollars. Indeed, if he only invests $25 a month, his money will grow to over $2 million!"

Satya shook her head in disbelief. "You mean that for a mere $50 a month your brother will be a millionaire when he retires? If I had only known, I would have started saving years ago."

"Amazing, isn't it?" said Sophia.

"Of course, a million dollars won't be worth as much in 40 plus years as it is now," Professor Braeburn admitted. "But it will be worth a lot more than the alternative, which is nothing. If my brother is smart, he will put more money away as he earns a larger salary. Starting to invest that early could realistically allow him to retire a multimillionaire."

"Before I answer Gregory's question about the 15% rate of return, let me give you one more example for older people like Satya who don't have 40 years before they retire," said Sophia. "Let's assume, Satya, that you and your husband are both 40 years old and are planning to retire at the age of 65. We don't want to get too personal, so let's pretend that you make $30,000 each, or $60,000 total per year. We will also assume that you follow the Golden 10% Rule and invest 10% of what you make, or $500 per month, at a 15% rate of return. At the age of 65, after the magic of compound interest, you will be left with $1,621,765. Not a bad nest egg after 25 years."

"Thanks," said Satya. "That's reassuring. My husband and I already invest several hundred dollars per month in mutual funds. From what you've shown me, if we keep investing, we should have a sizable sum set aside for retirement."

"I'm glad to hear it," said Professor Braeburn with a smile. "It sounds like you're already smart money managers."

"For the sake of our examples," he continued, "we've assumed that the person's income doesn't increase. But here's where the Golden 10% Rule gets exciting: For each pay increase, the rule forces you to set aside additional money based on the 10% rule. Your money will grow even more quickly when more money is added each month to your investment account."

"Take a look at this chart showing the magic of compound interest," said Sophia as she handed each student a copy. "You and any of your friends or family can use this chart to dream about how financially wealthy you can be someday."

$50 Invested Per Month (Tax Deferred)

	5%	10%	15%	20%
10th Year	$7,764	10,242	13,761	18,805
15th Year	13,364	20,724	33,425	55,785
20th Year	20,552	37,968	74,862	155,483
25th Year	29,775	66,342	162,176	424,264
30th Year	41,613	113,024	346,164	1,148,892
35th Year	56,805	189,832	733,859	3,102,466
40th Year	76,301	316,204	1,550,803	8,369,244
45th Year	101,322	524,125	3,272,251	22,568,320

$100 Invested Per Month (Tax Deferred)

	5%	10%	15%	20%
10th Year	$15,528	20,484	27,522	37,310
15th Year	26,729	41,447	66,851	111,570
20th Year	41,103	75,937	149,724	310,965
25th Year	59,551	132,683	324,353	848,529
30th Year	83,226	226,049	692,328	2,297,784
35th Year	113,609	379,664	1,467,718	6,204,932
40th Year	152,602	632,408	3,101,605	16,738,488
45th Year	202,644	1,048,250	6,544,503	45,136,640

$250 Invested Per Month (Tax Deferred)

	5%	10%	15%	20%
10th Year	38,821	51,211	68,804	94,024
15th Year	66,822	103,618	167,127	278,925
20th Year	102,758	189,842	374,310	777,413
25th Year	148,877	331,708	810,882	2,121,322
30th Year	208,065	565,122	1,730,820	5,744,459
35th Year	284,023	949,160	3,669,295	15,512,331
40th Year	381,505	1,581,020	7,754,014	41,846,220
45th Year	506,609	2,620,625	16,361,257	112,841,599

$500 Invested Per Month (Tax Deferred)

	5%	10%	15%	20%
10th Year	77,641	102,422	137,609	188,048
15th Year	133,644	207,235	334,253	557,850
20th Year	205,517	379,684	748,620	1,554,826
25th Year	297,755	663,417	1,621,765	4,242,643
30th Year	416,129	1,130,244	3,461,640	11,488,919
35th Year	568,046	1,898,319	7,338,590	31,024,661
40th Year	763,010	3,162,040	15,508,027	83,692,440
45th Year	1,013,219	5,241,251	32,722,513	225,683,198

"I wonder why we didn't learn any of this in school," remarked Elena, perplexed.

"It's a tragedy that schools and parents aren't teaching our children about the power of compound interest," Professor Braeburn responded. "Our great country is in trouble when it comes to managing money. It's a prosperous time, yet the credit card debt is higher than ever. I hope schools will take some of this simple practical knowledge and start teaching it to our kids."

Professor Braeburn turned to Sophia and pointed to his watch. She nodded, and he began, "I'm sorry we didn't get to your 15% rate of return question, but I think we've covered enough material for today. Your question happens to fall into the next wealth principle, which we'll discuss next week. We'll meet again next Saturday at 9:00 a.m.

"Remember, your homework for the coming week is to review your values and dreams lists and to put together your goals list. We taught you how to set goals; now it's up to you to follow through. Make sure you write these goals using the language of intention and action, that is, 'I intend to' or 'I will.' Maybe you could even imagine that you already possess what you desire."

Mark and Elena began gathering up their papers, while Satya read the dreams and values lists one more time.

"Thank you," said Gregory with genuine appreciation. "This first class has been an eye-opener for me."

"Yes, thank you, Professor Braeburn and Sophia," the others chimed in. "You've given us some real food for thought over the coming week."

"One more thing before we leave," Professor Braeburn added, handing around one last set of papers. "Here's a 'golden' list of influential authors, books, and materials. I recommend that during the next few months you spend time in the bookstore or library reading them. In fact, you should never quit learning. I believe that the authors and books on this list have some important insights to share."

The four students took the list, bade one another good-bye, and departed.

RECOMMENDED BOOKS ON SUCCESS, FULFILLMENT AND INTERNAL WEALTH

Jay Abraham, **Getting Everything You Can Out of All You've Got**

James Allen, **As A Man Thinketh**

Nancy Anderson, **Work with Passion**

Ken Blanchard, **One Minute Manager Series, Raving Fans, Everyone's a Coach, Gung Ho!, We are the Beloved, Mission Possible**

Victor Boc, **How to Solve All Your Money Problems Forever**

Stephan Bodian, **Meditation for Dummies, Living Yoga**

Richard Bolles, **What Color is Your Parachute**

Patti Breitman, **How to Say No without Feeling Guilty**

Les Browns, **Living Your Dreams**

Richard Carlson, **Don't Sweat the Small Stuff, Don't Worry, Make Money**

Jack Canfield, **Chicken Soup for the Soul Series**

Deepak Chopra, **Ageless Body, Timeless Mind, Seven Spiritual Laws to Success**

Stephen Covey, **Seven Habits of Highly Effective People**

Jim Donovan, **Handbook to a Happier Life**

Wayne Dyer, **See it When You Believe It, Your Erroneous Zone, Real Magic, Manifest Your Destiny, Wisdom of the Ages**

Beaty Eadie, **Embraced by the Light**

Mark Fisher, **The Instant Millionaire, The Millionaire's Secrets**

Victor Frankl, **Man's Search for Meaning**

Charles Garfield, **Peak Performance**

Charles Givens, **Super Self**

Stedman Graham, **You Can Make It Happen**

John Gray, **Men are From Mars, Women are From Venus**

Yitta Halberstam & Leventhal, **Small Miracles Series**

Mark Victor Hansen, **Chicken Soup for the Soul Series, The Miracle of Tithing, Dare to Win**

Connie Hatch, **How to Say No Without Feeling Guilty**
Louise Hay, **The Power is Within You, Gratitude: A Way of Life**
Napolean Hill, **Success Through a Positive Mental Attitude, Think and Grow Rich**
Sam Horn, **ConZentrate**
Phil Jackson, **Sacred Hoops**
Spencer Johnson, **Who Moved My Cheese, One Minute Manager**
Lawrence Leshan, **How to Meditate**
Og Mandino, **The Greatest Miracle in the World, The Greatest Success in the World, The Greatest Secret in the World, Mission: Success, A Better Way to Live**
Phil McGraw, **Life Strategies, Relationship Rescue**
Peter McWilliams & John-Rogers, **Life 101, Wealth 101**
Dan Millman, **Divine Interventions, The Way of the Peaceful Warrior**
Kent Nerburn, **Simple Truths**
Chuck Norris, **The Secret Power Within**
Norman Vincent Peale, **Power of Positive Thinking**
Scott Peck, **The Road Less Traveled**
Paul Pilzer, **Unlimited Wealth, God Wants You to be Rich**
Rick Pitino, **Success is a Choice**
James Redfield, **Celestine Prophecy**
Pat Riley, **The Winner Within**
Anthony Robbins, **Notes From a Friend, Awaken the Giant Within**
Bernie Siegel, **Love, Medicine, & Miracles, Peace, Love & Healing, Prescriptions for Living**
Howard Schultz, **Pour Your Heart Into It**
Steven K. Scott, **Simple Steps to Impossible Dreams, A Millionaire's Notebook**
Marsha Sinetar, **Do What You Love, The Money Will Follow**

Shunryu Suziki, **Zen Mind, Beginner's Mind**
Brian Tracy, **Maximum Achievement, Great Little Book Series, Success is a Journey**
Dennis Waitley, **The Winner's Edge, Empires of the Mind**
Stuart Wilde, **The Trick to Money is Having Some, The Little Money Bible, Miracles, The Force, Affirmations, The Quickening**
Marianne Williamson, **Return to Love**
Zig Ziglar, **See You at the Top, Over the Top**
Gary Zukav, **The Seat of Your Soul**

RECOMMENDED BOOKS ON PERSONAL FINANCE AND EXTERNAL WEALTH

Tod Barnhard, **The Five Rituals of Wealth, A Kick in the Assets**
David Chilton, **The Wealthy Barber**
George Clason, **The Richest Man in Babylon**
Charles Givens, **More Wealth Without Risk**
Kenneth Morris, **The Wall Street Journal Guides**
Suze Orman, **The 9 Steps to Financial Freedom, The Courage to Be Rich, You've Earned It, Don't Lose It**
Charles Schwab, **Charles Schwab's Guide to Financial Independence**
Eric Tyson, **Personal Finance for Dummies**

RECOMMENDED SPIRITUAL AND CLASSIC BOOKS

Bible
Bhagavad Gita
Mother Teresa
Confucius
Jalaluddin Rumi
Ralph Waldo Emerson
George Bernard Shaw

The Teachings of the Buddha
A Course in Miracles
Lao-tzu
Pantantjali
Henry David Thoreau
Mohandas Ghandhi
Martin Luther King, Jr

—I apologize to all the great authors and works that I have missed.

The following Saturday they all arrived at Professor Braeburn's office on time. After some opening chit-chat, they discussed the goal-setting assignment of the previous week, and then Gregory asked his 15% rate of return question again.

"I'm glad you raised that question again, Gregory," Sophia said warmly. "It's time for us to show you how you should be able to earn a 10%, 15%, or possibly even higher return on your money."

She turned to the board and wrote the seventh principle:

10 GOLDEN PRINCIPLES TO WEALTH

Internal Wealth

1. GOLDEN INTERNAL WEALTH

2. GOLDEN SPIRITUAL CONNECTION

3. GOLDEN GIVING AND RECEIVING

4. GOLDEN LEVERAGE WITH DREAMS, VALUES AND GOALS

5. GOLDEN INTENTION AND ACTION

External Wealth

6. GOLDEN 10% RULE

7. **GOLDEN OWNERSHIP—NOT LOANERSHIP**

"**E**arning a great rate of return boils down to 'golden' trust in American business and enterprise," she explained. "This country has prospered because of our free-enterprise system. The free-enterprise system works. Anyone who has ever placed diversified long-term faith in it has always succeeded. The best way, in fact maybe the only way, to capitalize on America's success is to own part of it."

"I like to look at it this way," said Professor Braeburn. "Historically, government bonds and savings accounts have yielded a dismal 4 to 5% interest per year. If history has taught us anything about investing for success, then we have learned that government bonds and savings accounts barely keep up with inflation. If you want your money to work for you, you can't afford to loan it to the bank or the federal government. Having said that, banks are getting much more creative these days.

Talk to your banker about checking accounts that earn interest. Many banks now have investment representatives who can help you out."

"I agree," said Sophia. "History has taught us over the years that owning part of America's businesses and/or real estate is by far the best way for investors to earn a nice long-term positive return.

"The naysayers will tell you to put your money in a safe government-backed bond. But I'm not sure that low-earning government-backed savings instruments are safe at all. When you're investing for the long term, I believe it's always safer to invest your money in good managed mutual funds or other ownership investment vehicles.

"If you put your money in a government bond or savings account, inflation will eat away at it and you'll effectively lose money. How safe can an investment be if it loses its value slowly? Savings accounts serve an important short-term purpose, but they shouldn't be used as a growth instrument.

"Let me give you another example that lends proof to this belief," the Guru continued. "Suppose you want to take your significant other out for dinner tonight. Let's agree that it will cost you $50. Now how will you be able to afford the same dinner 30 years from now? Assume that for the next 30 years our annual inflation rate averages 5%. In 30 years the same dinner will cost you about $223. If you spend all your money now and rely on social security when you retire, you may never be able to afford to go out for dinner in your retirement years.

"Here are your options. You can put your $50 in a savings account earning around 4% over 30 years. You would then be left with $166, or about 75% of the $223 price tag. Or you can invest the $50 for 30 years in one of my favorite mutual fund families, such as American Century or Janus. Assuming you're able to average the 15% return that I have received in the past, you'll have $4,377 in 30 years to take your wife out to dinner. In fact, you would be able to buy your wife a nice dinner every month for a year."

"But what if I want to go out to dinner today and not worry about the future?" Gregory asked.

"Good question. I have an option that will allow you to have the best of both worlds," replied Professor Braeburn. "Go out to dinner today, but find a way to spend only $25 instead of $50. Invest the other $25 in an account that will earn you a 15% rate of return. In 30 years you'll have $2,189 for a $223 dinner. This option allows you to have a nice dinner now and several nice dinners when you retire."

"The figures are quite impressive," said Mark thoughtfully. "Investing a little now can certainly make a huge difference in the future."

"You see," said Professor Braeburn, "we've basically just answered Gregory's question about receiving a 15% rate of return. To earn such a high yield, you need to be an owner in this country. We recommend mutual funds when you're just starting out, but there are many owner-ship opportunities available, such as real estate, stocks, and businesses."

After a moment of silence, Sophia said, "I'm reminded of a story in the New Testament (Matthew 25:14-30). A lord of three servants entrusts part of his wealth to each when he leaves for a faraway country. Two of the servants invest in ownership opportunities and are able to double the lord's wealth by the time he returns. The third servant is afraid of investments, so he buries the wealth in the ground to protect it. When the lord returns from his trip, he praises the servants who invested in ownership opportunities and earned him more. But he calls the third servant wicked and takes the money he buried and gives it to the others."

"I definitely get the point," said Gregory.

"Let me play the role of devil's advocate," challenged

Professor Braeburn. "The critics will tell you that history is no predictor of the future."

"You're right," Sophia agreed. "There will always be critics and doubters. It all boils down to your trust in the United States and our free enterprise system. If you believe in the future of our economy, then I think you should capitalize on it. As I said, the big winners in this world are the owners, not the loaners. One final point: There are some loaners that do very well because they loan money out at high rates of return. I consider these investors, not loaners."

"There are times, though, when people won't be interested in investment growth," Professor Braeburn added. "For example, five years before they retire, people generally become more interested in protecting their investments than in growing them. At such times, savings accounts or government bonds may be more appropriate than mutual funds or other ownership vehicles."

"Great point," Sophia agreed. "As always, you should seek the appropriate tax and investment experts to help you with your decision."

"As a naturalized citizen, I have tremendous faith in America and our approach to business," said Satya with enthusiasm. "It's so much more efficient and productive than the Indian system. That's why my husband and I moved here after we got married. We've done so much better financially than we could possibly have done in India."

"I have great faith in our system too—and I was born here!" said Elena. Everyone laughed. "I consider myself something of a futurist, and I predict that America will experience amazing technological, business, and even spiritual growth over the next century. I agree with you guys that the only way to share in this growth is through ownership."

"I agree with everything you've said so far, but I have two questions," said Mark. "First, you recommended mutual funds, but why shouldn't I just buy stocks? Second, you mentioned real estate. Doesn't it take a lot of time, money, and education to invest in real estate?"

"Good questions," responded Sophia. "Let me try to answer your question about real estate first. Real estate can be an incredibly profitable way to invest your money. By investing in land and real estate, you're building equity or ownership in something you can put your hands on."

"I've heard a statistic that I believe is fairly accurate," said Professor Braeburn. "Eighty-five percent of America's millionaires acquired their wealth at least in part through real estate."

"It's obvious that real estate has done well for many people," Sophia agreed. "I invest in real estate myself. But we're not going to discuss it in this class because I don't believe it's the best choice for beginners. Real estate investing takes more time, more research, and usually more money. I recommend that you practice mutual fund investing and the Golden 10% Rule for a few years before venturing into real estate."

"But if you're eager to learn more now, I suggest reading and studying everything you can get your hands on. I recommend Carleton Sheets's No Down Payment Program, which is often advertised on TV and can probably be found in many bookstores and libraries. You might also be able to take a real estate course at your local high school or college."

"Again, I must emphasize that I consider real estate investing an advanced money management technique," Sophia continued. "In a few years, when you've proven to me that you can follow the 10 principles that govern wealth, I will be much more interested in teaching you what I know about real estate investing."

"But what about the stock market?" Gregory persisted. "Can't people get rich buying and selling stock?"

"Yes, they can," Sophia agreed, "but it's difficult. Few people really understand good stock analysis, which is why mutual fund investing has become such an excellent alternative. Buying a mutual fund is like buying shares in a business corporation. With your investment, you gain access to a professional money manager who's trained in the analysis and selection of stocks. This manager manages a pool of money from investors large and small. You also get a relatively hands-off investment (meaning that you don't need to spend a lot of time monitoring it yourself) and incredible diversification. In return for this professional expertise you pay a small management fee."

"Mutual funds sound like the perfect investment," said Elena with excitement.

"Well, they're certainly not perfect," Sophia replied. "All ownership is subject to risk and fluctuation, and there are no guarantees. But, as I have said again and again, I feel safer having my money in a good managed growth mutual fund than I do in some government-backed savings vehicle."

"Remember also," added Professor Braeburn, "that mutual funds, like all ownership investments, are long-term. They will definitely fluctuate, and you can't let your emotions fluctuate with them. Despite the yearly fluctuations, the market has grown steadily in the long term, and I'm confident that this growth will continue.

If you're also confident that businesses will continue to grow and prosper in this country, it only makes sense to own and prosper from a piece of this growth."

"If you look at the average return on stocks and mutual funds in this country over the past 20 years, you'll see that, if the trends continue, it's realistic to expect a 10% rate of return. If you happen to pick one of the leading mutual funds, your return could be around 15% or more," Sophia concluded.

There was a brief moment of silence.

"Let's move on to another 'golden' technique, dollar cost averaging," Professor Braeburn suggested.

"Good idea," said Sophia, checking her watch. "Dollar cost averaging is one of the simplest and most exciting investment tools I have come across in my years of financial studies."

"What is your biggest fear about buying stocks or mutual funds?" Professor Braeburn asked the group.

"I guess I'm always worried that the stock market is too high or that it might crash when I buy," Gregory offered.

"Precisely," said Professor Braeburn. "When I started investing in mutual funds, I too was deathly afraid that the stock market might crash or correct itself. But Sophia showed me that the way I was investing I should celebrate a stock market correction or crash. I was dollar cost averaging and I didn't even know it."

"What do you mean?" asked Mark, puzzled.

"It isn't as complicated as it sounds. In fact, we alluded to it earlier," replied Sophia. "It's a system of consistently buying mutual fund shares at the same time each month with a consistent dollar amount."

"I thought investing in mutual funds every month was a way to get us to set money aside," said Mark .

"Yes, it does get you to set money aside to invest. But it also helps eliminate market timing risks," Sophia explained. "Perhaps an example will help clarify this point. Let's say you invest $200 a month in mutual fund XXX. The first month fund XXX is selling at $20 a share, so you buy 10 shares. The second month fund XXX drops to $10 a share, so you get 20 shares for your $200. The third month the market rebounds a little, and you buy your mutual fund shares at $15 each. For your $200 you receive 13.33 shares of mutual fund XXX. Now how many shares do you own?"

Before any of the students could respond, Sophia answered her own question. "After the third month you have a grand total of 43.33 shares of mutual fund XXX. Since the shares are now worth $15 a share, your total portfolio is worth $650."

She placed the following chart on the overhead:

DOLLAR COST AVERAGING			
Month	Shares	Price	Total $
1	10	$20.00	$200.00
2	20	$10.00	$200.00
3	13.33	$15.00	$200.00
Total Invested			$600.00
Total Value			
	43.33	$15.00	$650.00

"Wait a minute," Elena blurted out. "I only invested $600, the market and price dropped, and my mutual fund is still worth $50 more than I invested in total? That's incredible."

"Dollar cost averaging lets you profit in up, down, and volatile markets, as long as your investment escalates upward in the long term," Sophia continued. "As we said before, if you're patient with your money and the market grows over the long run, you can't lose. The genius behind this dollar cost averaging concept is that if the market goes down in the short run, you end up buying more shares for your money. When the market goes back up, as it always has, you will have purchased more shares that are now worth more money."

"I know from my own experience that this approach really works," Professor Braeburn assured them. "When Black Monday hit in 1987 and the market lost 500 points in one day, it remained low for many months. Since I continued to invest the same amount of money in mutual funds every month, I was able to purchase more shares for my money when the price was low. When the market rebounded and spiraled upward, I made a large profit because I now owned more shares. Eventually the price soared higher than ever, and I reaped an enormous return."

"This dollar cost averaging is an incredible way to invest," said Elena. "I'm going to get started this month."

"Totally," agreed Gregory. "It's awesome."

"What have we left out?" asked Sophia, turning toward Professor Braeburn with a smile.

"You're doing great," said the professor. "I think the next step is to discuss some of the rules for picking a good mutual fund.

"Before we do that, we need to talk about the 'golden' value of education and responsibility," mused Sophia. "Proper financial education is crucial in picking the best mutual funds. In fact, education and responsibility constitutes the eighth law of total wealth."

She turned toward the board and wrote:

10 GOLDEN PRINCIPLES TO WEALTH

Internal Wealth

1. GOLDEN INTERNAL WEALTH

2. GOLDEN SPIRITUAL CONNECTION

3. GOLDEN GIVING AND RECEIVING

4. GOLDEN LEVERAGE WITH DREAMS, VALUES AND GOALS

5. GOLDEN INTENTION AND ACTION

External Wealth

6. GOLDEN 10% RULE

7. GOLDEN OWNERSHIP—NOT LOANERSHIP

8. **GOLDEN EDUCATION AND RESPONSIBILITY**

It's vitally important for you as individuals to take responsibility for your future and educate yourself, not only about money, but about life. Both Professor Braeburn and I urge our students to take responsibility for their own lives."

"Unfortunately, many of us are taught in childhood to doubt and fear things in life. If, through education, we push past this fear and doubt and begin to take responsibility for our lives, we develop trust and knowledge. When we open ourselves to learning, we open ourselves to greatness, happiness, and fulfillment. Don't let others run your life. You must educate yourself and take responsibility for your life. Only by doing so can you live your life fully."

"Yes," agreed Sophia. "If you don't take responsibility for your life and your education, you're basically like a walking dead man. Who wants to live life the way

others say you must? Be your own person, educate yourself, and search inside for what feels right. Act on the
outside the way your insides tell you to act. I don't think
life is worth living if you're not in control of your life,
thoughts, and education."

"So you're saying that by educating myself and taking
responsibility for my life, I can build my internal wealth
and self-esteem and ultimately achieve the external
wealth of my dreams?" asked Gregory.

"Exactly," replied Sophia, smiling. " It's crucial to take
responsibility for your personal finances as well as every
other area of your life."

"It's actually a simple process," Professor Braeburn
added. "If you want to succeed at something, then study
it. You can begin by reading and studying in all areas of
your life that you want to improve.

"As far as personal finances, there are many magazines, books, and other materials available on the topic
of personal finance. The World Wide Web is exploding
with information and resources. Also, many colleges
now offer courses in personal financial management.

"No one's going to take care of you in this world, so
you have to take care of yourself," he continued. "Every
person has the responsibility to learn how basic personal finance works. You need to learn about insurance,

trusts, mortgages, money market accounts, stocks, etc. And it's especially important to learn about mutual funds.

"Once you start to understand personal finance and mutual fund investing, then you're better equipped to pick a good mutual fund. I predict that several dozen or more mutual funds will earn a 15% or higher rate of return over the next 20, 30, or 40 years. You need to educate yourself so that you can increase your odds of selecting one of these mutual funds.

"We'll recommend a couple of mutual fund families, such as American Century, Janus, and Fidelity, but generally we'll leave the selection up to you. Here's a list of our favorites," concluded Professor Braeburn, passing around copies.

GOLDEN MUTUAL FUND FAMILIES

1. AIM Advisors 800-347-1919
www.aimfunds.com

2. American Century 800-345-2021
www.americancentury.com

3. Fidelity .800-522-9297
www.fidelity.com

4. Janus 800-525-8983
www.janus.com

5. T. Rowe Price 800-231-8432
www.troweprice.com

6. Franklin/Templeton 800-223-2141
www.franklintempleton.com

7. Vanguard 800-662-7447
www.vanguard.com

8. IDS Mutual Funds 800-328-8300

OTHER SOURCES

1. Charles Schwab 800-225-8570
www.schwab.com

2. E-Trade . . . . .www.etrade.com

3. Merril Lynch . . . . .www.mldirect.com

4. Morningstar . . . . .www.morninstar.com

"We want to give you some guidelines that we follow in an attempt to pick the best mutual funds," said Sophia. "The first and most important key to selecting a good mutual fund is picking a good fund manager. As in business, some managers are better than others."

"Some people are management gurus and some are not," smiled Professor Braeburn, obviously referring to his popular book *The Golden Management Guru*.

"How do you sort out the good mutual fund managers from the average ones?" asked Satya.

"We recommend reading the top money and personal finance magazines, like *Money, Kiplinger's Personal Finance, Morningstar Mutual Funds, Forbes, Fortune, Business Week,* and *Worth,* as well as newspapers like *USA Today,* the *Wall Street Journal,* the *New York Times,* and many regional papers," replied Sophia. "You can go to the library to study them. All these publications do an outstanding job of monitoring and reporting on the performance of mutual funds and mutual fund managers. Also search the World Wide Web for vast resources on mutual funds."

"At least once a year, and generally more often, the print publications take a detailed look at average returns over various time periods and dig into the details of commissions, annual expense charges, and other important mutual fund statistics. As I mentioned, you can usually find most of these publications at your local library. The research needn't cost you a cent. Here's a list of the top publications and numbers if you want to purchase your own:"

MUTUAL FUND/PERSONAL FINANCE REFERENCES

Kiplingers 800-544-0155
www.kiplinger.com

Money Magazine 800-541-1000
www.money.com

Morningstar 312-696-6000
www.morninstar.com

Fortune 800-233-9003
www.pathfinder.com/fortune

Forbes 800-888-9896
www.forbes.com

Business Week. 800-635-1200
www.businessweek.com

Barron's. 800-544-0422
www.barrons.com

Worth. 800-777-1851
www.worth.com

Wall Street Journal. 800-369-2834
www.wsj.com

New York Times. 800-698-4937
www.nytimes.com

OTHER GOOD WEB SOURCES

Personal Fund	www.personalfund.com
Motley Fool	www.fool.com
Yahoo	http://quote.yahoo.com
Excite	www.excite.com
Investorama	www.investorama.com
MSN Money	http://investor.msn.com
FundAdvice	www.fundadvice.com
FundAlarm	www.fundalarm.com

"I look for growth mutual funds that have consistently out-performed the others for the past 15 to 20 years," Professor Braeburn confided. "If a mutual fund has consistently performed well over time with the same fund manager, then I'm inclined to believe that the fund manager has the expertise to continue to out-perform the others."

"I know what you mean about belief in past performance," agreed Gregory. "As you know, my father's a basketball coach. When his team is winning and the game is almost over, he makes sure to put in his best five free-throw shooters and ball handlers. The opposing team will usually attempt to foul his players to stop the clock. The opposing team's strategy is to make my father's team miss the pressure free throws and give themselves a chance to get the ball back, score, and win.

"My father's logic is simple. Knowing the opposing team is going to foul, why should he use a player who in the past has made about 50% of his free throws when he can use someone who tends to shoot with about 75% accuracy from the free-throw line? Although he has confidence in all his players, he tends to follow the percentages and statistics of past performance. His plan isn't perfect because everyone can have a bad game, but he believes that past performance is the best indicator of future performance."

"I like your dad's logic," Sophia said, laughing.

"Great analogy," Professor Braeburn agreed. "Knowledge is the key."

"I like to repeat what Einstein once said about knowledge," Sophia added. "I'm paraphrasing, but he essentially said that we can't solve our problems with the same knowledge that created the problems. If you had more or the right knowledge, you wouldn't have produced the problem in the first place. So you need to take responsibility and educate yourself.

"Just as I tell people to take responsibility for their inner wealth and spiritual growth, I also want them to control what's happening to their money. Mutual fund investing is fairly simple; if people would apply themselves just a little, they could take control of their financial future.

"Before we move on to Wealth Principle 9, I have one final point to make about golden education and responsibility," continued Sophia. "After you spend a little time studying mutual funds and personal finance, you can start setting aside your Golden 10% of what you make. But first you need to study your financial situation to determine the type of account in which your mutual funds should be placed.

"The best place to put your 10% is in some type of

tax-deferred retirement account. A tax-deferred account allows your money to grow tax deferred until you take it out. The second important advantage of a tax-deferred account is that it forces you to leave it there. Generally, you can't take the money out until you're 59$\frac{1}{2}$ without incurring a severe penalty."

"There are several different options for retirement accounts," interjected Professor Braeburn.

"Yes," Sophia agreed. "Your employer may offer you some type of pension plan, or what is called a 401K. If these aren't offered, you might need to set up an individual retirement account (IRA). Like anything, there are rules and regulations that you must follow, so research these with an expert. Most of these programs are as simple as filling out a few papers and picking the mutual funds where you want your money placed. You can ask your employer for information on these programs, and you can get the mutual funds phone numbers from Morningstar or the other financial publications we listed.

"You can also find information on retirement accounts in the books we recommended last week."

"OK, let's take a little break," said Professor Braeburn, "and then we can cover our last two laws for achieving total wealth."

The four students stood up, stretched, and left the room while the professor and Sophia conferred. After about ten minutes, the seminar once again convened, and the Golden Guru opened the session by writing the ninth principle on the board:

10 GOLDEN PRINCIPLES TO WEALTH

Internal Wealth

1. GOLDEN INTERNAL WEALTH

2. GOLDEN SPIRITUAL CONNECTION

3. GOLDEN GIVING AND RECEIVING

4. GOLDEN LEVERAGE WITH DREAMS,
   VALUES AND GOALS

5. GOLDEN INTENTION AND ACTION

External Wealth

6. GOLDEN 10% RULE

7. GOLDEN OWNERSHIP—NOT LOANERSHIP

8. GOLDEN EDUCATION AND RESPONSIBILITY

9. **GOLDEN EXPENSE CONTROL**

"I suppose this is the part where you lecture us on the merits of budgeting, thrift, and comparison shopping," teased Mark, seeing expense control on the marker board.

"Ya," said Professor Braeburn in a mock German accent. "Ve vill teach you to vatch and record every dime you ever spend." Laughter filled the room.

"The attitude behind your comment is precisely the reason that we won't initially teach you about budgeting and thrift," commented Sophia. "I used to preach budgeting, thrift, and other financially stringent measures, but 99% of my students passionately resisted. After all, this is America, land of the free! I learned that no one wants to be told how to spend their money or be forced to watch over every cent they spend."

"Charles Givens, an influential personal finance coach, feels the same way about budgeting as most of us do," said Professor Braeburn. "After years of study on the subject, Givens summed it up perfectly when he said, 'The two most difficult personal promises to keep are certainly budgeting and dieting. Neither produces instant rewards or the positive feedback so necessary for continued motivation. Budgeting is a plan requiring self-sacrifice now for some vague reward sometime in the not-so-foreseeable future. Budgeting never worked for me and it probably won't work for you.'"

"Whew!" said Mark, still teasing. "What a relief!" Everyone laughed again.

"Instead of budgeting, which, as you can see, doesn't sit well with most people, we teach 'golden control,'" said Sophia, smiling. "Golden expense control involves one simple principle. I'll teach you this principle in a moment, but first let's look at how the Golden 10% Rule eliminates some of the need to watch every expense to the penny.

"I am a bit different from Professor Braeburn. I have my golden 10% transferred directly from my checking account to my mutual fund each month. As long as you're saving your golden 10% first, you can do what you want with the rest of your money. Of course, you must remember not to spend more than you have."

"So you're saying that as long as I invest my 10% I can

spend the rest as I choose as long as I don't spend more than I have," asked Elena.

"Yes," Professor Braeburn replied, "that's basically what we're saying. But now that we've clarified that spending your discretionary income is up to you, I must emphasize that using golden control and common sense with the money will allow you to get ahead faster."

"Now I'd like to teach you my one simple 'control your expense' doctrine," said Sophia.

"Everyone can remember this," Professor Braeburn affirmed. "After many years of financial study, this rule still serves as the only guideline I use to control my expenses."

After erasing one of the boards, Sophia wrote:

GOLDEN EXPENSE CONTROL DOCTRINE

Think before you spend.

"When I tell you to think before you spend, I don't mean that you should watch every dollar," Sophia explained. "I just want you to keep in mind what's important to you. Look over your values and goals lists regularly. If something isn't important to you, then don't buy it."

"Basically, Sophia is saying that you must live within your means and pay some attention to how you spend your discretionary income," said Professor Braeburn.

"Of course, you should treat yourself to nice things once in a while," added Sophia. "Just be smart with your money.

"I teach an advanced budgeting course," she continued, "that shows in detail how you can affect your financial life with a little thrift. But this advanced course is only for those who are really interested. You'll do just fine in this world if you save your golden 10% and put a little thought into how you spend the rest."

"I really appreciate the simplicity of your teachings," said Satya. "You make everything seem so clear and straightforward."

"Thanks, Satya," said Professor Braeburn. "We've both spent a great deal of time studying what really works in wealth building and distilling it down to a few essential principles. As Sophia told you last week, wealth building laws are simple and effective if you just apply them."

"Last week I promised to share with you some of the mistakes I made as I learned the ten principles that govern wealth. Well, unfortunately I didn't follow the rule of think before you spend, and I abused my credit cards. My spouse and I purchased some frivolous items and did some unnecessary travel. Before I knew it we had maxed out our credit limit on three cards. It took us a long time to finally pay those cards off."

"There's also a huge burden of guilt that goes along with accumulating debt," said Sophia. "Useless debt seems to generate a negative state of mind. It's difficult to attract wealth when you're spending carelessly. It's better to think before you buy and only buy those things you really need or value. You want money to flow to you, not away from you."

"There are two books I recommend on getting money to flow to you instead of away from you," said Professor Braeburn. "One is *The Trick To Money is Having Some* by Stuart Wilde; the other is *How To Solve All Your Money Problems Forever* by Victor Boc. These books will help you understand the psychology of money. Both authors know the steps it takes to be a money magnate."

"Perhaps you can tell our little group what else you did to pay off your credit cards," Sophia suggested.

"Gladly," Professor Braeburn agreed. "The other trick I used to eliminate the debt caused by poor choices was to follow the 10th principle that governs wealth. At the time I was very unhappy with my career. I felt unproductive and frustrated with my situation. I finally decided to follow my heart and create the life I had always dreamed about."

The Professor turned to the board and wrote:

10 GOLDEN PRINCIPLES TO WEALTH

Internal Wealth

1. GOLDEN INTERNAL WEALTH

2. GOLDEN SPIRITUAL CONNECTION

3. GOLDEN GIVING AND RECEIVING

4. GOLDEN LEVERAGE WITH DREAMS, VALUES AND GOALS

5. GOLDEN INTENTION AND ACTION

External Wealth

6. GOLDEN 10% RULE

7. GOLDEN OWNERSHIP—NOT LOANERSHIP

8. GOLDEN EDUCATION AND RESPONSIBILITY

9. GOLDEN EXPENSE CONTROL

Conclusion

10. GOLDEN MISSION

"**A**t last," beamed Sophia, "we've arrived at the concluding principle. "

She seems to be glowing more than usual, Gregory pondered. *She must be really passionate about this principle.*

"We all have unique and special talents that make us stand out from the rest of the world. It's our life mission not only to seek peace and love, but also to seek out that something special in ourselves that we can offer to humanity. Each of us has a 'golden' mission or passion that, if pursued, will give us a sense of accomplishment and bliss because we've done something worthwhile, something that will make our universe a more positive and loving place. Shakespeare put it this way: 'To thine own Self be true.'"

"In other words, you must find a career that you're passionate about," said Professor Braeburn, "a career that fits your life's mission. In doing what you love, you'll usually take care of your current financial problems. When people go after their golden mission, the money often follows."

"Creating wealth starts with finding what you love to do and molding it in a manner that creates value for yourself and others," agreed Sophia.

"You must take your ideas, thoughts, and inspirations and turn them into knowledge, products, or services that will have an impact on the world. By doing this you'll not only be loving life, but you'll be creating wealth. With wealth you can affect the lives of millions of people and stimulate our economy. The faster wealth goes around the economy the more it's available in products and other opportunities. You owe it to yourself and the world to find what you're passionate about and turn it into your career.

"Many years ago, when I was in college, I became fascinated by the study of personal finance," Sophia continued. "After a lull in my corporate career when I didn't know what I wanted to do next, I decided to turn money into my life's work. It was the best decision I ever made because it allowed me to create an enormous net worth within a couple of years."

"I was a struggling single mother working an entry-level management job to get by. When I decided to follow my dream and teach people about personal finance, the money started to pour in. First I worked for several years as a financial planner in a large investment company. I became passionate about personal finance and helping the company grow. My excitement and commitment to the company inspired the people around me. As my passion grew, so did my income. Because I cared about my company and my job, I received a steady stream of raises and bonuses.

"Eventually, I set out on my own and created my current financial planning empire. Five or six years after I began to follow my golden mission, I reached the famed millionaire status. I'm not saying everyone will become a millionaire—maybe it's not even that important. But I *am* saying that if you get passionate about your career or develop your passion into a job, more often than not your checkbook will grow."

"Let me corroborate Sophia's story with two of my own," said Professor Braeburn. "The first story is mine. When I followed my dream and became a college professor, I started to earn a good income. Then when I followed my life mission to write books, the money flowed to me in abundance. But enough about me."

"My second story is about Mildred Robbins Leet and her late husband Glen. They both had a dream.

They had already spent many years in public service helping people but had a passion to make a significant impact on poverty. With $1,000 they started the Trickle Up organization in New York City. They planned to be funded by corporations, individuals, and foundations and would use these donations to offer small grants to those at poverty levels. These grants would be used to help individuals launch businesses as a way to survive and grow their internal and external wealth. The Leets knew that often it only takes a little help for people to move themselves out of poverty.

"Trickle Up has succeeded by helping over 85,000 small businesses around the world. Since families are involved in most of these businesses, it is estimated that they have helped as many as 500,000 people and the number runs into the millions if you count the products produced and sold to customers around the world. The Leets are a great example of this book. They increased their own spirituality and self-worth, became masters at giving and receiving, created leverage with dreams, values and goals, took action and followed their Golden Mission. Isn't it amazing how one couple has impacted millions by following many of the Golden Principles in this book?" The Professor and Sophia looked at the students.

"Incredible," said Mark as the others nodded.

"Everyone has specialized talents, skills, and abilities," Sophia continued. "You must devise a method or plan to use these talents to add value or quality to people's lives. Look back over your dreams, goals, and values lists. What is it about you that you love and that can become your life mission? If you investigate carefully, you can definitely find your deeper purpose in life."

"I believe in this principle of a golden mission," said Gregory. "But other than reviewing my dreams, goals, and values, what else can I do to help me find my mission?"

"As in discovering internal wealth, the process of finding your mission is often as important as the mission itself," Sophia advised. "It doesn't happen instantaneously. You must begin to read, reflect, write, pray, meditate, and use any of the other methods and activities people use to enlighten themselves to meaning.

"Most of the time your life mission can be found in what you're most enthusiastic about," she continued. "Interestingly enough, the word 'enthusiasm' is derived from the Greek, *en theos,* which means 'God in us.' Often what excites you the most is what the universe and your spirit are screaming at you to do.

"I'd like to recommend two excellent books on this topic. The first is *Do What You Love and the Money Will Follow* by Marsha Sinetar. Marsha has changed thousands of lives by getting people to follow their passion. The second is *What Color Is Your Parachute?* by Richard Bolles. We'll talk some more about Richard's work in a few minutes.

"Since you're into basketball," Professor Braeburn said to Gregory, "I have a great example about following your passion that I know you'll appreciate. I'm sure the rest of you will enjoy it as well. It's the life, mission, and passion of Phil Jackson, the head coach of the Los Angeles Lakers and the former coach of the six-time world-champion Chicago Bulls."

Professor Braeburn took a book from his desk and opened it to a marked page. "In his autobiography *Sacred Hoops,*" began the professor, holding the book up for the class to see, "Phil says that his two greatest passions are basketball and the spirituality of being in the moment. He has been able to enjoy both of his passions by coaching and teaching. In other words, he's living the life of his dreams.

"Phil writes, 'In basketball, as in life, true joy comes from being fully present in each and every moment, not just when things are going your way. . . . Basketball is an expression of life, a single, sometimes glittering thread, that reflects the whole. Like life, basketball is messy and unpredictable. It has its way with you, no matter how hard you try to control it. The trick is to experience each moment with a clear mind and an open heart. When you do that, the game—and life—will take care of itself.'"

"That's awesome," remarked Gregory. "I knew Phil Jackson was a great coach, but I didn't realize he had such a spiritual attitude toward life. I definitely must read his book."

"Yes," said Sophia, smiling. "Often we have to dig beyond our thoughts into our heart, soul, and spirit to find our purpose and mission in life."

"Richard Bolles agrees," said Professor Braeburn. "He teaches that determining our mission in life is a learning process with three major steps. First, we have to seek out our spirit, the universal energy or God in us. Second, we need to do whatever we can, day by day, step by step, to make this world a better place by following the spirit or God-force within us and around us. Finally, we need to exercise our talents or our greatest gifts. What has the world given us? What do we enjoy? What can we do that will create the most value and good in this world?

"It's important to remember that some people won't find their true calling or golden mission right away," Professor Braeburn advised. "Patience and practice are important. We need to take one step at a time while following our heart. Some of us may not be able to see where life is leading us or what our ultimate purpose will be. In the end, our ultimate purpose may turn out to be the journey itself—what we learned and did while we were searching for our purpose."

"You know," offered Satya, "what you're teaching us about finding our golden mission sounds remarkably similar to what you taught us about finding internal wealth and developing a spiritual connection."

"Good point," replied Sophia. "They're intimately connected. Growing, learning, living, and loving all involve following the universal spiritual energy and love that is in each of us."

"We all have a responsibility to identify and pursue our true calling or golden mission in life," added Professor Braeburn. "And in pursuing our mission we need to try to live every moment with love, joy, fun, passion, and enthusiasm.

"Why not make the right choice to find and follow your golden mission?" asked Sophia, looking at each student in turn. "Why not make the choice that will bring you true satisfaction? Go after everything you enjoy. Create a career full of meaning. Make choices that will cause the positive energy in this world to multiply. If everyone followed their mission, we would all be amazed by how extraordinary this world could be."

"I agree wholeheartedly," said Professor Braeburn. "There's no reason not to follow your heart—that's what life is all about. If you want to feel like a million bucks and have a million bucks, then you need to follow the ten principles we've outlined for you. Most important, you need to find your golden mission in life and use it to help others."

"Well, I think we've come to the end of our seminar," said Sophia with a radiant smile. "I urge you to apply these ten principles and transform your life, just as Professor Braeburn and I have transformed ours. As the Nike ad says, 'Just do it.' You'll be glad you did."

10 GOLDEN PRINCIPLES TO WEALTH

Internal Wealth

1. GOLDEN INTERNAL WEALTH

2. GOLDEN SPIRITUAL CONNECTION

3. GOLDEN GIVING AND RECEIVING

4. GOLDEN LEVERAGE WITH DREAMS, VALUES AND GOALS

5. GOLDEN INTENTION AND ACTION

External Wealth

6. GOLDEN 10% RULE

7. GOLDEN OWNERSHIP—NOT LOANERSHIP

8. GOLDEN EDUCATION AND RESPONSIBILITY

9. GOLDEN EXPENSE CONTROL

Conclusion

10. GOLDEN MISSION

"We've truly enjoyed having you in our little seminar." Professor Braeburn said, looking at each student in turn. "Keep us posted on your progress. We wish you all good luck and bon voyage."

"Thank you so much," said Elena, moved by the professor's warm words. "I've learned so much more than I ever imagined I would."

"Yes, thank you," said Satya and Mark. "We'll keep in touch."

"I never dreamed when I called you several weeks ago that I would have the good fortune to stumble on such an amazing seminar," said Gregory. "I'll never forget the wise words of advice you've shared with us these past two weeks."

With warm hugs and enthusiastic words of appreciation, the four students ventured forth once again into the world, equipped with the means to enrich their lives beyond their wildest dreams.

Golden Praisings

I would like to give a public praising to the many people who directly or indirectly helped me with this book through love, friendship, support, feedback, inspiration and knowledge.

Tracy Roadifer, my spouse and best friend, for loving me and our boys unconditionally and allowing me to take the risks that I must take in life.

Wayne Roadifer, my father, for his love, support and incredible example of education, hard-work and success.

Pam Roadifer, my mother, for her love, support and for developing my confidence and independence. A special thanks for your graphical design help.

Bryan Roadifer, my brother and friend, for his love and his teaching me through example the ability to take risks and live life at the fullest.

Frank Young, for friendship, spiritual growth, and supporting the entreprenurial spirit.

Judy Young, for helping me take care of Tracy and the boys.

Friends (aka Cornell/Bama Boyz), *Seth Anderson, Alex Armatas, Greg Freyenberger, Dan Junkins, Jason Krzewinski, Shayne Marker, Daryn Mcbeth, Colin McPherron, and Doug Timmer,* for the highest quality friendship anyone could ever ask for. May we continue to make our friendship a priority.

Keith Brownfield and Mike Easton for high quality friendship and mentorship in my business career.

Professor James Stout and Professor Clyde Nue for their great teaching, mentorship, early reading, and support.

Elbert Belish, Penny Vance, Gilbert Martel, Scott Lillie and Terry Radcliffe for their support and early readings of the book.

Roadifer, Belish, Young, and Lawerence families for their love and support.

Ruth Susott and *Sandy Brownfield* for their friendship and proofreading help.

Stephan Bodian, whose incredible editing took my stilted and awkward manuscript and improved it immensly.

Carol Susan Roth for her recommendations.

Sue Knopf, for her superb layout and design of this book.

Ken Blanchard, for your *One Minute Manager* series and *Personal Excellence* program that was the trigger or spark that initiated the creation of this book.

Wayne Dyer and Anthony Robbins, my favorite gurus, whose work more than any have driven me to new levels of internal and external success.

Stephen Covey, Richard Bolles, Deepak Chopra, Og Mandino, Napolean Hill, Jack Canfield, Mark Victor Hansen, Les Brown, Dennis Waitley, Tod Barnhardt, James Allen, David Chilton, Steven Scott, Jay Abraham, Louise Hay, Brian Tracy, John Gray, Richard Carlson, Marsha Sinetar, Paul Pilzer, Bernie Siegel, Mark Fisher, Stuart Wilde, Zig Ziglar, Suze Orman, Peter McWilliams, and Oprah Winfrey for their incredible writing, speaking, and work to improve people's life. You have all had a significant and positive impact on my life. Thank you for following your golden missions.

Charles Givens, for creating a personal finance crusade.

David McClelland, for your pioneering work in motivation and success that I see sprinkled in so many others' work.

Bud Gardner, Dan Poynter and the entire Maui Writer's Retreat for the friendship, knowledge and contacts that have helped create *The Golden Guru.*

John Bratton and *John V. Riffe* for their catagloging and technical library help

Cornell College, for a great education from an outstanding school.

University of Montana, for a great education from an outstanding university.

About the Author

Mr. Roadifer is a successful young spouse, father, writer, speaker, and consultant. He is happily married to his high school sweetheart Tracy and they have two beautiful sons.

He has successfully owned two businesses, is a published author, personal and business consultant, speaker, and has risen to hold a top management position in a growing multi-million-dollar insurance company, all before the age of 30. Recently he has started the Golden Group, which offers seminars, consulting, private consultation, and leadership training to individuals and businesses across the country.

Mr. Roadifer has studied personal, psychological, spiritual and personal financial growth for over 13 years. He holds undergraduate bachelor degrees in Economics/Business (finance emphasis) and Psychology (personal development emphasis) from Cornell College and a Masters of Business Administration (M.B.A.) from the University of Montana. He has also completed more than 100 additional seminars and courses in success, leadership, personal development, spiritual growth, business and money.

Mr. Roadifer has written *The Golden Guru: 10 Spiritually Based Principles to Success, Fulfillment, and Wealth*. Work is also started on an entire Golden Book Series including *The Golden Health Guru, The Golden Management Guru, The Golden Relationship Guru,* and *The Golden Marketing Guru.*

Mr. Roadifer would love to speak, train or present a seminar for you or your organization. If interested, call him at 406-652-8254.

Would You Like to Be Part of the
Golden Guru Book Series?

Greg Roadifer and his Golden Group Associates are compiling short stories on real world Golden Gurus. If you know a true story about a real Guru that should be shared with the world please write us and tell us about him or her. We are looking for short stories about individuals who are inspiring and uplifting.

Write to: Greg Roadifer
             GoldenHouse Publishing
             P.O. Box 23307
             Billings, MT 59104

Fast Order Form

Golden Guru Books can be purchased from most local bookstores, amazon.com and barnesandnoble.com, or order direct from the GoldenHouse Publishing Group.

☎   *Call:*   1-406-652-8254, Have credit card ready

✉   *Mail:*   GoldenHouse Publishing, P.O. Box 23307,
                  Billings, MT 59104

www   *Web:*   www.goldenguru.com

💻   *Email:* goldenguru@imt.net

Please send the following books:

☐   1 for $14.95 plus shipping - *THE GOLDEN GURU: 10 Spiritually Based Principles to Success, Fulfillment and Wealth.*

☐   3 for $39.95 plus shipping - *THE GOLDEN GURU: 10 Spiritually Based Principles to Success, Fulfillment and Wealth.*

Name _____

Address _____

City _____ State_____ Zip _____

Telephone _____

Email _____

Please Add Shipping

US: $4.00 for first book and $2.00 for each additional book.
International: $9.00 for first book and $5.00 for each additional.

Payment

☐ Cheque   ☐ Credit Card: __ Visa   __ MasterCard

Card Number _____

Name on Card _____

Expiration Date _____/_____

Fast Order Form

Golden Guru Books can be purchased from most local bookstores, amazon.com and barnesandnoble.com, or order direct from the GoldenHouse Publishing Group.

☎   *Call:*   1-406-652-8254, Have credit card ready

✉   *Mail:*   GoldenHouse Publishing, P.O. Box 23307, Billings, MT 59104

www   *Web:*   www.goldenguru.com

🖳   *Email:* goldenguru@imt.net

Please send the following books:

☐   1 for $14.95 plus shipping - *THE GOLDEN GURU: 10 Spiritually Based Principles to Success, Fulfillment and Wealth.*

☐   3 for $39.95 plus shipping - *THE GOLDEN GURU: 10 Spiritually Based Principles to Success, Fulfillment and Wealth.*

Name _____

Address _____

City _____ State_____ Zip _____

Telephone _____

Email _____

Please Add Shipping
   US: $4.00 for first book and $2.00 for each additional book.
   International: $9.00 for first book and $5.00 for each additional.

Payment

☐ Cheque   ☐ Credit Card: __ Visa   __ MasterCard

Card Number _____

Name on Card _____

Expiration Date ____/_____

Fast Order Form

Golden Guru Books can be purchased from most local bookstores, amazon.com and barnesandnoble.com, or order direct from the GoldenHouse Publishing Group.

☎   *Call:*   1-406-652-8254, Have credit card ready

✉   *Mail:*   GoldenHouse Publishing, P.O. Box 23307, Billings, MT 59104

www   *Web:*   www.goldenguru.com

⌨   *Email:* goldenguru@imt.net

Please send the following books:

☐   1 for $14.95 plus shipping - *THE GOLDEN GURU: 10 Spiritually Based Principles to Success, Fulfillment and Wealth.*

☐   3 for $39.95 plus shipping - *THE GOLDEN GURU: 10 Spiritually Based Principles to Success, Fulfillment and Wealth.*

Name _____

Address _____

City _____ State_____ Zip _____

Telephone _____

Email _____

Please Add Shipping

US: $4.00 for first book and $2.00 for each additional book.
International: $9.00 for first book and $5.00 for each additional.

Payment

☐ Cheque   ☐ Credit Card: __ Visa   __ MasterCard

Card Number _____

Name on Card _____

Expiration Date _____/_____

Recommended Golden Guru Publishing Resources

Small publishers rely on professionals when producing books. We know that with the Golden Guru book we used some of the best in the business. Consider these professionals for your next book project.

Dan Poynter's Para Publishing

They have a treasury of resources on book writing, producing, publishing, selling and promoting. Their Web site has over 500 pages of helpful, valuable information. See http://ParaPub.com. For a free information kit, call 800-PARAPUB or go to the Web site.

Graffolio Design and Typesetting

Our aim is to make your book interior look great! Since 1987 we've designed and typeset more than 90 books as well as brochures, logos, maps, forms and more. Our services include designing the interior of your book; laying out pages and providing you with laser proofs; copy-editing if you request it; scanning or creating artwork; and sending computer files for your book to your printer. Call Sue at 608-784-8064 or e-mail graffolio@compuserve.com for more information.

Stephan Bodian

He is a freelance editor, writer, and writing consultant specializing in spirituality, psychology, and alternative health. Author of three books, including *Meditation For Dummies* (IDG Books), he was editor-in-chief of the magazine *Yoga Journal* for 10 years and is currently editor of the Psychology section for Broadcasthealth.com. He is also a psychotherapist in private practice in Marin County and San Francisco. He can be reached at 415-451-7133; stephan@wenet.net.

Robert Howard Graphic Design

With over 15 years of experience and hundreds of book covers, Robert Howard Graphic Design is one of the best in the business. See www.rhgraphicdesign.com. Call Robert at 970-225-0083 or e-mail rhgd@verinet.com.

NOTES

NOTES